D0014475

Reflective Teaching in
Second Language Classrooms

CAMBRIDGE LANGUAGE EDUCATION
Series Editor: Jack C. Richards

This new series draws on the best available research, theory, and educational practice to help clarify issues and resolve problems in language teaching, language teacher education, and related areas. Books in the series focus on a wide range of issues and are written in a style that is accessible to classroom teachers, teachers-in-training, and teacher educators.

In this series:

Agendas for Second Language Literacy *by Sandra Lee McKay*

Reflective Teaching in Second Language Classrooms
by Jack C. Richards and Charles Lockhart

Educating Second Language Children: The whole child, the whole curriculum, the whole community *edited by Fred Genesee*

Reflective Teaching in Second Language Classrooms

Jack C. Richards
City University of Hong Kong

Charles Lockhart
City University of Hong Kong

CAMBRIDGE
UNIVERSITY PRESS

60105059

Published by the Press Syndicate of the University of Cambridge
The Pitt Building, Trumpington Street, Cambridge CB2 1RP
40 West 20th Street, New York, NY 10011–4211, USA
10 Stamford Road, Oakleigh, Melbourne 3166, Australia

© Cambridge University Press 1994

First published 1994

Printed in the United States of America

Library of Congress Cataloging-in-Publication Data

Richards, Jack C.
Reflective teaching in second language classrooms / Jack C.
Richards and Charles Lockhart.
p.   cm. – (Cambridge language education)
Includes bibliographical references and index.
ISBN 0–521–45181–7 (hc). – ISBN 0–521–45803-X (pbk.)
1. Language and languages – Study and teaching.   I. Lockhart,
Charles, (date). II. Title. III. Series.
P51.R485   1994
418′.007 – dc20   93–4305
                                                              CIP

A catalog record for this book is available from the British Library

ISBN 0–521–45181–7   hardback
ISBN 0–521–45803-X   paperback

Contents

Series editor's preface   ix
Preface   xi

Introduction: Teacher development through exploring classroom processes   1

1 Approaches to classroom investigation in teaching   6

Journals   7
Lesson reports   9
Surveys and questionnaires   10
Audio or video recording of lessons   11
Observation   12
Action research   12
Appendixes   16

2 Exploring teachers' beliefs   29

The source of teachers' beliefs   30
Beliefs about English   32
Beliefs about learning   34
Beliefs about teaching   36
Beliefs about the program and the curriculum   38
Beliefs about language teaching as a profession   40
Follow-up activities   42
Appendixes   44

3 Focus on the learner   52

Learner belief systems   52
Cognitive styles   59
Learning strategies   63

Follow-up activities   67
Action research case study #1: Learner strategies   69
Appendixes   72

4   Teacher decision making   78

Planning decisions   78
Interactive decisions   83
Evaluative decisions   87
Follow-up activities   90
Action research case study #2: Negotiating course content with
learners   91
Appendixes   93

5   The role of the teacher   97

The nature of roles   97
Roles reflecting institutional factors   98
Roles reflecting a teaching approach or method   101
Roles reflecting a personal view of teaching   104
Cultural dimensions of roles   107
Follow-up activities   109
Action research case study #3: Renegotiating teacher–learner roles
to increase student motivation   110

6   The structure of a language lesson   113

Openings   114
Sequencing   118
Pacing   122
Closure   124
Follow-up activities   125
Action research case study #4: Transitions during lessons 126
Appendixes   129

7   Interaction in the second language classroom   138

The teacher's action zone   138
Interactional competence   141
Learner interactional patterns   144
Grouping arrangements   146
Follow-up activities   154
Action research case study #5: Grouping arrangements in the
classroom   157
Appendixes   159

8 The nature of language learning activities   161

   Types of language learning activities   162
   Dimensions of language learning activities   167
   Follow-up activities   173
   Action research case study #6: Student performance on learning
   activities   178
   Appendix   181

9 Language use in the classroom   182

   How teachers modify their language   182
   Teachers' questions   185
   Feedback   188
   Learner language use in the classroom   193
   Follow-up activities   199
   Action research case study #7: Error correction   200

Epilogue   202
References   205
Index   215

Series editor's preface

A recent trend in second language teaching is a movement away from "methods" and other "external" or "top down" views of teaching toward an approach that seeks to understand teaching in its own terms. Such an approach often starts with the instructors themselves and the actual teaching processes, and seeks to gain a better understanding of these processes by exploring with teachers what they do and why they do it. The result is the construction of an "internal" or "bottom up" view of teaching. The approach is often teacher initiated and directed because it involves instructors observing themselves, collecting data about their own classrooms and their roles within them, and using that data as a basis for self-evaluation, for change, and hence for professional growth.

It is this "reflective approach" to teaching, as it applies to second language classrooms, that Charles Lockhart and I have illustrated in this book. Reflective teaching goes hand-in-hand with critical self-examination and reflection as a basis for decision making, planning, and action. The book focuses on a number of important dimensions of teaching, including teachers' and learners' beliefs, teacher decision making, and teachers' and learners' roles. It introduces the significance of each issue along with related theory and research and then presents a number of exploratory tasks and activities, such as journal writing, peer observation, and action research, which teachers can carry out in their own classrooms. Each chapter thus promotes the role of reflection, self-inquiry, and self-evaluation as a means of professional development.

Jack C. Richards

Preface

Reflective Teaching in Second Language Classrooms is designed for use in pre-service and in-service teacher education programs offering a teaching practicum or courses on classroom observation, theories of teaching, or language teaching methods and approaches. Instructors can use the book as a basis for either individual or collaborative teacher development activities, including peer observation, self-evaluation, program evaluation, and action research.

Each chapter presents an important dimension of teaching and poses questions that form the basis for classroom observation and investigation as well as critical reflection. The suggested small-scale investigative tasks can be carried out by teachers or student teachers in a variety of classroom situations.

Chapter 1 provides an introduction to classroom investigation procedures, including teaching journals, lesson reports, surveys and questionnaires, audio and video recording, observation, and action research. Chapter 2 examines how teachers' ideas and beliefs about teaching and learning can influence their classroom practices. Chapter 3 deals with learners' beliefs, goals, and attitudes and how these influence their learning styles and strategies. Chapter 4 discusses the thinking processes underlying teaching and considers three areas of decision-making: planning, interactive, and evaluative decisions. Chapter 5 examines the roles teachers perform in their institutions and their own classrooms, the responsibilities these roles create, and how they contribute to the instructor's teaching style. Chapter 6 explores how teaching events are structured and how different structuring choices can influence the coherence and dynamics of a lesson. Chapter 7 focuses on the nature of classroom interaction, the interaction patterns typical of second language classrooms, and ways in which teachers can influence these patterns. Chapter 8 examines lessons in terms of the activities teachers use to achieve their instructional goals along with decisions to consider when planning and using activities. Chapter 9 focuses on the linguistic dimensions of classroom interaction and looks at the relationship between language use in the classroom and language acquisition.

The chapters have been ordered for convenience of presentation. With the exception of Chapter 1, they may be used in any order. Chapter 1 should be read first since it describes the procedures for reflective teaching which will be used throughout the book. The remaining chapters are self-contained discussions of important aspects of teaching and can be used in various ways depending on whether the book is used with pre-service or in-service teachers. Questions in each chapter have been included to stimulate further reflection on the topics discussed. Where possible, these questions take into account teachers in both pre-service and in-service programs. At the end of each chapter are suggestions for follow-up activities, such as journal writing, peer observation, classroom investigation, or examples of action research. Throughout the book, quotes from learners and teachers, as well as transcripts from classroom data, are used to illustrate the issues discussed. When no source is given, the examples have been provided by teachers attending courses or workshops which we conducted.

This book was written to provide material and activities for pre-service and in-service courses on language teaching which we have conducted in various countries including the United States, Brazil, Hong Kong, and Japan. We are grateful to the participants in these courses, particularly the students at City University of Hong Kong, for trying out many of the activities presented here and for allowing us to visit their classrooms and explore their teaching with them.

Jack C. Richards
Charles Lockhart

Introduction: Teacher development through exploring classroom processes

Asking questions about teaching

This book explores the nature of teaching in second language class-rooms, and introduces teachers and teachers-in-training to techniques which can be used to explore teaching. The book aims to develop a reflective approach to teaching, that is, one in which teachers and student teachers collect data about teaching, examine their attitudes, beliefs, assumptions, and teaching practices, and use the information obtained as a basis for critical reflection about teaching. Critical reflection involves asking questions such as the following, which form the focus of the individual chapters of the book.

- How can I collect information about my own teaching? (Chapter 1)
- What are my beliefs about teaching and learning, and how do these beliefs influence my teaching? (Chapter 2)
- Where do these beliefs come from? (Chapter 2)
- What kind of teacher am I? (Chapter 2)
- What beliefs do my learners hold about learning and teaching? (Chapter 3)
- How do these beliefs influence their approach to learning? (Chapter 3)
- What learning styles and strategies do my learners favor? (Chapter 3)
- What kind of planning decisions do I make use of? (Chapter 4)
- What kind of on-the-spot decisions do I make while I teach? (Chapter 4)
- What criteria do I use to evaluate my teaching? (Chapter 4)
- What is my role as a teacher? (Chapter 5)
- How does this role contribute to my teaching style? (Chapter 5)
- How do my learners perceive my role as a teacher? (Chapter 5)
- What form or structure do my lessons have? (Chapter 6)
- How do I communicate goals to my learners? (Chapter 6)

- How effectively do I utilize learning opportunities within a lesson? (Chapter 6)
- What kinds of interaction occur in my classroom? (Chapter 7)
- What interactional styles do my learners favor? (Chapter 7)
- What kind of grouping arrangements do I use and how effective are they? (Chapter 7)
- What kind of learning activities do I employ? (Chapter 8)
- What is the purpose of these activities? (Chapter 8)
- What patterns of language use occur when I teach? (Chapter 9)
- How do I modify my language to facilitate teaching and learning? (Chapter 9)
- What opportunities do learners have for authentic language use in my lessons? (Chapter 9)

In asking and answering questions such as these, teachers are in a position to evaluate their teaching, to decide if aspects of their own teaching could be changed, to develop strategies for change, and to monitor the effects of implementing these strategies.

Such questions are often asked by teachers when describing problems they face in their teaching. In discussing these kinds of questions, teachers often point out that many conventional approaches in teacher development rarely help them find answers which will give them practical help with their problems. In-service workshops designed to improve teaching skills often have only short-term effects and rarely involve teachers in an ongoing process of examining their teaching.

In order to answer questions like those listed here, it is necessary to look objectively at teaching and reflect critically on what one discovers. The information obtained through the process of exploring teaching can be useful in a number of ways. It can help achieve a better understanding of one's own assumptions about teaching as well as one's own teaching practices; it can lead to a richer conceptualization of teaching and a better understanding of teaching and learning processes; and it can serve as a basis for self-evaluation and is therefore an important component of professional development.

Discussion

1. Which of the questions listed in this section are of greatest interest to you?
2. What other questions do you think are important to ask about teaching?
3. Compare your answers to these questions with those of a colleague.

The assumptions underlying this book

This book takes teachers and teachers-in-preparation through a number of activities that focus on different dimensions of second or foreign language teaching. The questions it explores are not linked to a particular method or view of teaching, since teachers work in very different kinds of situations (e.g., some with beginning learners and others with advanced students), with different kinds of content (e.g., some teach reading while others teach writing or speaking), with different teaching methods and approaches, and have different amounts of experience and skill (some may be in pre-service programs and others may be experienced teachers). The book does not set out to tell teachers what effective teaching is, but rather tries to develop a critically reflective approach to teaching, which can be used with any teaching method or approach.

The techniques introduced for exploring teaching are based on the following assumptions about the nature of teacher development.

1. *An informed teacher has an extensive knowledge base about teaching.* Teaching is a complex, multidimensional activity. The teacher who has a more extensive knowledge and deeper awareness about the different components and dimensions of teaching is better prepared to make appropriate judgments and decisions in teaching.

2. *Much can be learned about teaching through self-inquiry.* For many teachers, classroom visits by supervisors are the main source of feedback on their teaching. While comments of a supervisor or other outside visitor can be a useful source of information about one's teaching, teachers themselves are in the best position to examine their own teaching. Rather than drawing on experts' opinions, theories, or external sources of knowledge as an impetus for change or development, the approach in this book involves teachers in collecting information about their teaching either individually or through collaborating with a colleague, making decisions about their teaching, deciding if initiatives need to be taken, and selecting strategies to carry them out.

3. *Much of what happens in teaching is unknown to the teacher.* Teachers are often unaware of the kind of teaching they do or how they handle many of the moment-to-moment decisions that arise. This is seen in the following comments, which were made by teachers after watching videotapes of their own lessons.

I had no idea I did so much talking and didn't let students practice.
My pacing was terrible. I didn't give students enough time to practice one task before going on to another.

I did a bad job on the group work exercises. The students didn't un-
  derstand what they were supposed to do.
I seemed to ignore half the students in the class.

Since many things happen almost simultaneously during a lesson, it is
sometimes difficult for teachers to be aware of what happens in classrooms and why. The activities used throughout this book are designed to
help make teaching more visible, through collecting and examining data
on many dimensions of teaching.

4. *Experience is insufficient as a basis for development.* While experience is a key component of teacher development, in itself it may be
insufficient as a basis for professional growth. Many aspects of teaching
occur day in and day out, and teachers develop routines and strategies for
handling these recurring dimensions of teaching. However, research
suggests that, for many experienced teachers, many classroom routines
and strategies are applied almost automatically and do not involve a great
deal of conscious thought or reflection (Parker 1984). Experience is the
starting point for teacher development, but in order for experience to play
a productive role, it is necessary to examine such experience systemat-
ically. For this, specific procedures are needed: these are introduced in
Chapter 1.

5. *Critical reflection can trigger a deeper understanding of teaching.*
Critical reflection involves examining teaching experiences as a basis for
evaluation and decision making and as a source for change (Bartlett
1990; Wallace 1991). It involves posing questions about how and why
things are the way they are, what value systems they represent, what
alternatives might be available, and what the limitations are of doing
things one way as opposed to another.

Teachers who are better informed as to the nature of their teaching are
able to evaluate their stage of professional growth and what aspects of
their teaching they need to change. In addition, when critical reflection is
seen as an ongoing process and a routine part of teaching, it enables
teachers to feel more confident in trying different options and assessing
their effects on teaching.

  These assumptions reflect the fact that if teachers are actively involved
in reflecting on what is happening in their own classrooms, they are in a
position to discover whether there is a gap between what they teach and
what their learners learn. This process of reflection is a particular kind of
research, which Cross (1988: 3) describes as

the study by classroom teachers of the impact of their teaching on the
students in their classrooms. The basic premise of classroom research is that

teachers should use their classrooms as laboratories to study the learning process as it applies to their particular disciplines; teachers should become skilful, systematic observers of how the students in their classrooms learn.

The systematic exploration of classroom processes forms the theme of this book.

Discussion

1. Review the five assumptions about teacher development listed in this section. Do you agree with these assumptions? What assumptions do you hold about the process of teacher development? What factors have influenced your development as a teacher, or are likely to influence your development in the future?
2. If you are already teaching, can you identify changes you have made in your own teaching or in your approach to teaching? These could be changes in your view of yourself as a teacher, your approach to students, or the method or techniques you use. Why did you make these changes and how did they come about?

1 Approaches to classroom investigation in teaching

The assumption underlying this book is that in every lesson and in every classroom, events occur which the teacher can use to develop a deeper understanding of teaching. Teachers sometimes fail to exploit these events, letting momentum of all the other events of the day take precedence. And yet these experiences can serve as the basis for critical reflection, if teachers can find ways to capture the thoughts of and reactions to these events, as well as ways to gather fuller information about the events themselves. From this basis, teachers can develop strategies for intervention or change, depending on their needs. In this chapter, a number of simple procedures are introduced that can be used to help teachers investigate classroom teaching. Each procedure has advantages and limitations, and some are more useful for exploring certain aspects of teaching than others. The reader will have to decide which procedures are useful and for what purposes.

The procedures discussed here will be referred to throughout the book and consist of:

1. *Teaching journals.* Written or recorded accounts of teaching experiences.
2. *Lesson reports.* Written accounts of lessons which describe the main features of the lessons.
3. *Surveys and questionnaires.* Activities such as administering a questionnaire or completing a survey, designed to collect information on a particular aspect of teaching or learning.
4. *Audio and video recordings.* Recordings of a lesson, or part of a lesson.
5. *Observation.* Tasks completed by a student teacher observing a cooperating teacher's class, or peer observation (i.e., tasks completed by a teacher visiting a colleague's class).
6. *Action research.* Implementation of an action plan designed to bring about change in some aspect of the teacher's class with subsequent monitoring of the effects of the innovation.

Journals

A journal is a teacher's or a student teacher's written response to teaching events. Keeping a journal serves two purposes:

1. Events and ideas are recorded for the purpose of later reflection.
2. The process of writing itself helps trigger insights about teaching. Writing in this sense serves as a discovery process.

Many different topics from classroom experiences can be explored through journal writing, for example:

Personal reactions to things that happen in the classroom or in the school.
Questions or observations about problems that occur in teaching.
Descriptions of significant aspects of lessons or school events.
Ideas for future analysis or reminders of things to take action on.

Some teachers prefer to audiotape their responses to teaching, keeping an "audio journal" rather than a written journal.

Bartlett (1990: 209–10) gives the following suggestions for what to write about (or record).

Our writing will be about our routine and conscious actions in the classroom; conversations with pupils; critical incidents in a lesson; our personal lives as teachers; our beliefs about teaching; events outside the classroom that we think influence our teaching; our views about language teaching and learning.

Appendix 1 at the end of this chapter contains a list of reflection questions that can be used to provide a focus for journal writing. Readers should review these questions as they read the book.

The following procedures are recommended for keeping a journal (Bailey 1990; Porter et al. 1990; Walker 1985).

1. Make entries on a regular basis, such as once or twice a week, or even daily if possible. It may be useful to spend five or ten minutes after a lesson to write about it or record it.
2. Review your journal entries regularly. What might not have been obvious when written or recorded may later become apparent. As you review your journals, ask yourself questions like these:

What do I do as a teacher?
What principles and beliefs inform my teaching?
Why do I teach the way I do?
What roles do learners play in my classes?
Should I teach differently?

Keeping a journal can also be beneficial when one or more colleagues share their journals and meet regularly to discuss them (Brock, Yu, and Wong 1992). Appendix 2 shows a case study of three teachers involved in collaborative journal writing.

The following is an example of a teacher's journal entry.

Today I gave my class a reading activity which focused on skimming. I gave them an article to read called "Study Paints Grim Picture" and asked them to skim through the article to identify the social problems mentioned. After a few minutes, I checked the answers and asked the students to number the paragraphs. They had to find the paragraphs which contain information on each of the social problems. Then I checked the answers and explained some difficult vocabulary. Then I gave one handout which contained five paragraphs and another handout which contained five headlines. Students had to match them.

Afterthoughts

Timing again was a problem. I originally planned to check the answers of the matching exercise, but there was no time.

Less time should have been spent on explaining expressions as it defeated the objective of my lesson – skimming.

I should have allocated a specific amount of time to practice skimming.

I should have opened the lesson with a discussion of social problems so that students could compare their answers with what they found in the article.

This teacher's journal entry reveals how she has used her journal: to describe how she presented a teaching activity, to identify some concerns she had about the lesson, and to remind her of alternative procedures to use in the future. It also reinforces the unique function of journal writing – it enables a teacher to examine teaching in a way that is unavailable through other means.

Discussion

1. Have you or any of your colleagues ever kept a journal? What kind of journal was it and for what purpose? What did you learn from your journal-keeping experience?
2. What kinds of issues and concerns are useful to focus on when keeping a journal about your teaching?
3. Who do you think is the most suitable audience for your teaching journal? How does the intended audience affect the way you write or record your journal?

Lesson reports

A lesson report is a structured inventory or list which enables teachers to describe their recollections of the main features of a lesson. The purpose of a lesson report is to give the teacher a quick and simple procedure for regularly monitoring what happened during a lesson, how much time was spent on different parts of a lesson, and how effective the lesson was. Whereas a lesson plan describes what a teacher intends to do during a lesson, a lesson report describes what actually happened from the teacher's point of view.

While a lesson report is not a completely accurate account of what occurred during a lesson, it often serves as a useful record of many important features of the lesson and can hence be used to help monitor the teacher's teaching. Published lesson report forms are available for many aspects of ESL lessons (Pak 1985).

To be effective, lesson report forms should be prepared by a teacher or group of teachers to match the goals and content of the particular course they are teaching. The following procedures are recommended in preparing self-report forms:

1. First, identify in as much detail as possible the philosophy underlying the course and the different kinds of teaching activities, procedures, and resources that you expect to use in the course. For example, a group of teachers teaching a grammar class would first discuss their approach to the teaching of grammar, clarify their assumptions about the goals of the course, and identify the kinds of classroom activities, procedures, and resources they plan to use.
2. Next, prepare a lesson report form. The grammar teachers discussed earlier, for example, would prepare a checklist which could be used to collect information about how grammar was presented and practiced during a lesson. The checklist should be pilot tested to improve its design. (See Appendix 3 for a sample form.)
3. Use the lesson report form on a regular basis to record the activities, procedures, and resources used throughout the course.
4. Meet periodically to review and compare lesson reports with those of other teachers teaching the same course. As you do so, discuss any differences that are emerging in the way you teach the class and the reasons for these differences. If necessary, rethink and modify the teaching strategies and materials you are using. Alternatively, you may wish to monitor your own teaching using self-report forms, thus gathering important information that will be useful the next time you teach the same course.

An alternative approach to lesson reporting is simply for the teacher to spend a few minutes after a lesson writing answers to questions such as the following:

- What were the main goals of the lesson?
- What did the learners actually learn in the lesson?
- What teaching procedures did I use?
- What problems did I encounter and how did I deal with them?
- What were the most effective parts of the lesson?
- What were the least effective parts?
- Would I do anything differently if I taught the lesson again?

Discussion

1. What kind of information do you think should be included in a lesson report?
2. What are the advantages and disadvantages of doing a lesson report in the form of: (a) a checklist and (b) a response to questions like those above?

Surveys and questionnaires

Some aspects of teaching and learning can be investigated through carrying out a survey or administering a questionnaire. For example, a teacher may wish to investigate students' attitudes toward group work. A questionnaire is administered to the class which asks students to indicate how useful they find group work activities, what they think they learn from them, and for what content areas or skills they think group work is most appropriate. Surveys and questionnaires are useful ways of gathering information about affective dimensions of teaching and learning, such as beliefs, attitudes, motivation, and preferences, and enable a teacher to collect a large amount of information relatively quickly. Appendix 4 is a questionnaire which elicits learners' preferences for different kinds of learning activities. Examples of different kinds of surveys and questionnaires are discussed in later chapters of the book.

Discussion

1. What are some aspects of teaching or learning that could usefully be investigated using a questionnaire?
2. How could the information from question 1 be used? Who should have access to this information?

Audio or video recording of lessons

The advantage of the preceding procedures is that they are relatively easy to carry out. However, a disadvantage is that they obtain subjective impressions of teaching and by their nature can capture only recollections and interpretations of events and not the actual events themselves. Hence other procedures are also necessary. The fullest account of a lesson is obtained from an actual recording of it, using an audio cassette or video recorder. With a cassette recorder or a video camera placed in a strategic place in a classroom, much of what happened in a lesson can be recorded.

One of the advantages of recording a lesson is that it allows choice of focus – this could be the teacher (if the teacher wears a microphone) or a particular group of students (if the recorder is placed close to them). An additional advantage is that the recording can be replayed and examined many times and can capture many details of a lesson that cannot easily be observed by other means, such as the actual language used by teachers or learners during a lesson. Schratz (1992: 89) comments:

Audio-visual recordings are powerful instruments in the development of a lecturer's self-reflective competence. They confront him or her with a mirror-like "objective" view of what goes on in class. Moreover, class recordings which are kept for later use, can give a valuable insight into an individual teacher's growth in experience over years.

However, recording a lesson also has limitations. For example, the presence of a recording device may be disruptive; recording devices often have a limited range (e.g., they may capture only students seated in the front row); and reviewing a recording is time consuming. Schratz (1992:89) points out:

Setting up the equipment for a lecture's recording and going through the various analyzing phases requires a lot of time. For this reason, this type of activity can never become an activity continued on a day-to-day basis. It will only be applied on special occasions.

Discussion

1. Listen to an audio recording of one of your lessons or of a teacher's lesson. Did you learn anything unexpected from it?
2. In what ways could the presence of a video camera change the dynamics of the classroom? How serious a problem is this and how can it be minimized?
3. What aspects of a lesson can be captured through an audio recording and what cannot?

Observation

Observation involves visiting a class to observe different aspects of teaching. Throughout this book observation is suggested as a way of gathering information about teaching, rather than a way of evaluating teaching. In many language programs, teachers are often reluctant to take part in observation or related activities since observation is associated with evaluation. Thus in order for observation to be viewed as a positive rather than a negative experience, the observer's function should be limited to that of gathering information. The observer should not be involved in evaluating a teacher's lesson. Throughout this book, two kinds of observation will be referred to – observation by student teachers of a cooperating teacher's class, and peer observation, in which one teacher observes a colleague's class. Guidelines for carrying out observation by student teachers are given in Appendix 5. Guidelines for carrying out peer observation are given in Appendix 6.

Discussion
1. What is your experience of observing someone's class or having someone observe your class? Was it a positive or negative experience? Why?
2. What kinds of useful information about teaching could be gathered through observation?

Action research

Action research is used in this book to refer to teacher-initiated classroom investigation which seeks to increase the teacher's understanding of classroom teaching and learning, and to bring about change in classroom practices (Gregory 1988; Kemmis and McTaggart 1988). Action research typically involves small-scale investigative projects in the teacher's own classroom, and consists of a number of phases which often recur in cycles:

Planning
Action
Observation
Reflection

For example, the teacher (or a group of teachers):

1. Selects an issue or concern to examine in more detail (e.g., the teacher's use of questions).

2. Selects a suitable procedure for collecting information about the topic (e.g., recording classroom lessons).

3. Collects the information, analyzes it, and decides what changes might be necessary.

4. Develops an action plan to help bring about the change in classroom behavior (e.g., develops a plan to reduce the frequency with which the teacher answers questions).

5. Observes the effects of the action plan on teaching behavior (e.g., by recording a lesson and analyzing the teacher's questioning behavior) and reflects on its significance.

6. Initiates a second action cycle, if necessary.

The following example illustrates this approach to action research.

[A Japanese teacher of English] wanted to increase the amount of English he was using in the classroom. To do this he first investigated how much he used his native tongue (Japanese) during his teaching and for what purposes he was using it. He checked three tapes recorded at different times over a two-week period and first listened to them just to determine the proportion of English to Japanese he was using. It was about 70% English, 30% Japanese. He then listened to the tapes again to find out the purposes for which he was using Japanese. He found he was using Japanese for two main purposes: classroom management and giving feedback. He then drew up a plan to reduce the amount of Japanese he was using for these two purposes. He first consulted a guide to the use of English in the classroom (Willis 1981) and familiarized himself with English expressions that could be used for classroom management and feedback. He wrote out a set of expressions and strategies on 3″ by 5″ cards, and put these in a conspicuous place on his table. These served not only to remind him of his plan but also helped him remember some of the expressions he wanted to use. Each day he would place a different card on top of the pile. He then continued recording his lessons and after a few weeks checked his tapes. His use of Japanese had declined considerably.   (Richards 1990: 131)

While action research may be an inevitable follow-up to classroom investigation, it is not necessarily so, since many of the activities discussed throughout this book are beneficial for their own sake and need not necessarily be linked to the notion of change or improvement. Further guidelines for conducting action research are given in Appendix 7.

Discussion

1. What would be some suitable issues or topics for action research in a class you are observing or teaching?
2. What kind of information would you need to collect to investigate each issue in more detail?
3. Select one of these issues and develop an action plan for it.

The approaches described in this chapter are just some of the ways in which teachers can become involved in what has been referred to as "critically reflective teaching" or "exploratory teaching." (For other approaches see Allwright 1988; Allwright and Bailey 1991; Fanselow 1987; Nunan 1989a; Woodward 1991.) What distinguishes these approaches to classroom investigation from other investigative strategies is that they are intended to complement the kinds of things teachers normally do as they teach, rather than impose additional chores on teachers. Furthermore, they let teachers themselves (rather than outsiders) decide which aspects of teaching they wish to explore and which procedures they prefer to use.

Discussion

1. Read the following situations. Which of the procedures discussed in this chapter would be most appropriate for gathering information about it: teaching journal, lesson reports, surveys and questionnaires, audio and video recording, or observation? What are the advantages and disadvantages of the procedure you selected?
   a. You are concerned about your students' attitudes toward English and toward language learning. You try to promote positive attitudes toward learning English. You wish to find out what your students' attitudes are and whether they change throughout the duration of a language course.
   b. You are very conscientious about planning your lessons, but somehow they never seem to go according to plan. You rarely have time to get through all the material that you had planned. You want to find out why this is happening.
   c. You are concerned about one of your students who always avoids sitting near the front of the class. This student seems to be paying attention, but rarely participates actively in lessons. You are not sure why. Since you have a large class, it is difficult for you to monitor individual students. You want to find out what this student's attitude is

toward the class, how the student approaches learning, and whether the student is benefiting from the class.

d. You have been teaching English to elementary students for several years, and colleagues point out that you have developed a special kind of "teacher's English." You want to investigate whether this is true, what these features are, and whether it helps or hinders your teaching.

e. You have been experimenting with a process approach for teaching writing (i.e., one in which you encourage students to go through a number of stages when completing a writing task, from planning to drafting to reviewing and revising). You want to find out if students actually find this approach useful and whether they use it on writing assignments outside of class.

2. Which of the issues in question 1 would be suitable for action research? Discuss how an action research project could be developed.

Appendix 1: Reflection questions to guide journal entries

Questions about what happened during a lesson

Questions about your teaching
1. What did you set out to teach?
2. Were you able to accomplish your goals?
3. What teaching materials did you use? How effective were they?
4. What techniques did you use?
5. What grouping arrangements did you use?
6. Was your lesson teacher dominated?
7. What kind of teacher-student interaction occurred?
8. Did anything amusing or unusual occur?
9. Did you have any problems with the lesson?
10. Did you do anything differently than usual?
11. What kinds of decision making did you employ?
12. Did you depart from your lesson plan? If so, why? Did the change make things better or worse?
13. What was the main accomplishment of the lesson?
14. Which parts of the lesson were most successful?
15. Which parts of the lesson were least successful?
16. Would you teach the lesson differently if you taught it again?
17. Was your philosophy of teaching reflected in the lesson?
18. Did you discover anything new about your teaching?
19. What changes do you think you should make in your teaching?

Questions about the students
1. Did you teach all your students today?
2. Did students contribute actively to the lesson?
3. How did you respond to different students' needs?
4. Were students challenged by the lesson?
5. What do you think students really learned from the lesson?
6. What did they like most about the lesson?
7. What didn't they respond well to?

Questions to ask yourself as a language teacher

1. What is the source of my ideas about language teaching?
2. Where am I in my professional development?

3. How am I developing as a language teacher?
4. What are my strengths as a language teacher?
5. What are my limitations at present?
6. Are there any contradictions in my teaching?
7. How can I improve my language teaching?
8. How am I helping my students?
9. What satisfaction does language teaching give me?

Appendix 2: An example of collaborative journal writing

This study was initiated by three English language teachers as a means of recording and reflecting on their teaching.

Diary keeping has been reported to have important benefits for teachers in that it can provide access to hidden affective variables that influence the way teachers teach and students learn. Other advantages are that it provides a means of generating questions and hypotheses, is a tool for reflection, requires only a simple recording method and does not rely on an outside observer in the classroom.

Most published diary studies in second language classrooms research have reported individual diaries, but these teachers considered that there were advantages in keeping diaries together, reflecting on and talking about their own as well as the diaries of others.

Each teacher planned to keep diaries of two of their classes per week over a ten week term.

Entries were made for a range of different classes including business, technical and supplementary English. In writing the diary entries, teachers attempted to combine the narration of classroom events with their reflections of those events. They did not narrow their focus to a few issues.

To maximise the effects of interactions among the three diarists, diary keeping was coupled with written responses and group discussions. These three steps offered a kind of triangulation process. Each teacher gave their diary entries to the others to read and they wrote brief responses to each others' entries before their discussion period. Discussions were audio-taped and transcribed.

At the end of term, diary entries, written responses and transcripts were analyzed to determine how these three interacted and what issues occurred most frequently.

Often written responses were characterized by questions or requests for more information from the diarist. Written responses were also used to request that a particular issue or question be considered during the Friday afternoon discussions, and for drawing together mutual concerns in the diary entries.

Another interesting phenomenon arising from the interaction of diary entries, written responses and weekly discussions was the pattern in which issues were developed: from a more local, micro-level (actual classroom events) to a more general macro-level.

Conflicting emotions were expressed: diary keeping was seen as valuable in providing insights and in raising awareness to some extent, but at the same time the discipline of diary keeping was a burden on time and energies of participants.

On the positive side, diary keeping enabled the teachers to focus on several important issues and the issues, questions and concerns that arose from the project served as an agenda for future classroom research. It also enabled teachers to gain inside perspectives on other teachers' experiences.

In future teachers considered that the focus should be on a few salient issues to allow participants the opportunity to investigate in depth a few issues of common interest rather than attempting to explore many issues at the same time. Finally it is essential that a substantial block be made available to devote to the discipline of diary keeping and sharing.

(Reprinted with permission from D. Kember, M. Kelly (1992), *Using Action Research to Improve Teaching*, p. 21, Hong Kong: Hong Kong Polytechnic.)

Appendix 3: Lesson report form for a grammar lesson

1. The main focus in today's lesson was:
   a. Mechanics (e.g., punctuation and capitalization)
   b. Rules of grammar (e.g., subject-verb agreement; pronoun use)
   c. Communicative use of grammar (e.g., correct use of past tense forms in a narrative)
   d. Other

2. The amount of class time spent on grammar work was:
   a. The whole class period
   b. Almost all of the class period
   c. Less than that (_____ minutes)

3. I decided what grammar items to teach:
   a. According to what was in the textbook
   b. According to what was in the course syllabus
   c. Based on students' performance on a test
   d. Based on students' errors in oral and written work
   e. Other

4. I taught grammar by:
   a. Explaining grammar rules
   b. Using visual aids
   c. Presenting student errors
   d. Giving students practice exercises from a textbook
   e. Giving students practice exercises that I designed

5. When assigning student work on grammar, I had students:
   a. Study rules of grammar
   b. Practice exercises orally in class
   c. Practice exercises orally in the language lab
   d. Do exercises for homework
   e. Do exercises based on errors noted in their writing
   f. Go over each other's homework or classwork
   g. Keep a personal record of the errors they make
   h. Do sentence-combining exercises
   i. Create sentences or paragraphs using specific grammar rules or sentence patterns
   j. Identify and correct grammar errors in writing samples
   k. Identify and correct grammar errors in their own writing
   l. Identify and correct grammar errors in other students' writing
   m. Other

Appendix 4: Student questionnaire to investigate learning preferences

STUDENT QUESTIONNAIRE

HOW DO YOU LEARN BEST?

Example:
I like to learn by listening to songs.   no   a little   good   best

1.	In English class, I like to learn by reading.	no	a little	good	best
2.	In class, I like to listen and use cassettes.	no	a little	good	best
3.	In class, I like to learn by games.	no	a little	good	best
4.	In class, I like to learn by conversations.	no	a little	good	best
5.	In class, I like to learn by pictures, films, video.	no	a little	good	best
6.	I want to write everything in my notebook.	no	a little	good	best
7.	I like to have my own textbook.	no	a little	good	best
8.	I like the teacher to explain <u>everything</u> to us.	no	a little	good	best
9.	I like the teacher to give us problems to work on.	no	a little	good	best
10.	I like the teacher to help me talk about my interests.	no	a little	good	best
11.	I like the teacher to tell me all my mistakes.	no	a little	good	best
12.	I like the teacher to let me find my mistakes.	no	a little	good	best
13.	I like to study English by myself (alone).	no	a little	good	best
14.	I like to learn English by talking in pairs.	no	a little	good	best
15.	I like to learn English in a small group.	no	a little	good	best
16.	I like to learn English with the whole class.	no	a little	good	best
17.	I like to go out with the class and practise English.	no	a little	good	best
18.	I like to study grammar.	no	a little	good	best
19.	I like to learn many new words.	no	a little	good	best
20.	I like to practise the sounds and pronunciation.	no	a little	good	best
21.	I like to learn English words by <u>seeing</u> them.	no	a little	good	best
22.	I like to learn English words by <u>hearing</u> them.	no	a little	good	best
23.	I like to learn English words by <u>doing</u> something.	no	a little	good	best
24.	At home, I like to learn by reading newspapers, etc.	no	a little	good	best
25.	At home, I like to learn by watching TV in English.	no	a little	good	best
26.	At home, I like to learn by using cassettes.	no	a little	good	best
27.	At home, I like to learn by studying English books.	no	a little	good	best
28.	I like to learn by talking to friends in English.	no	a little	good	best
29.	I like to learn by watching, listening to Australians.	no	a little	good	best
30.	I like to learn by using English in shops/CES trains...	no	a little	good	best

(Reprinted with permission from K. Willing (1988), *Learning Styles in Adult Migrant Education*, pp. 106–7, Adelaide, Australia: National Curriculum Resource Center.)

STUDENT QUESTIONNAIRE cont...

31. When I don't understand something in English,
    I ask someone to explain it to me.   no   sometimes   often

32. If something in English is too difficult for me,
    I try to listen to some <u>part</u> of it.   no   sometimes   often

33. I watch people's faces and hands to help me
    understand what they say.   no   sometimes   often

34. When I'm reading - if I don't understand a word, I
    try to understand it by looking at the <u>other</u> words. no   sometimes   often

35. When I am not in class, I try to find ways to use
    my English.   no   sometimes   often

36. I am happy to use my English even if I make
    mistakes.   no   sometimes   often

37. I think about what I am going to say before I speak.   no   sometimes   often

38. If I don't know how to say something, I <u>think</u> of
    a way to say it, and then I try it in speaking.   no   sometimes   often

39. When I am speaking English, I <u>listen</u> to my
    pronunciation.   no   sometimes   often

40. If I learn a new word, I try to put it into my
    conversation so I can learn it better.   no   sometimes   often

41. If someone does not understand me, I try to
    say it in a different way.   no   sometimes   often

42. I like the sound of English.   no   sometimes   often

43. I try to find my special problems in English,
    and I try to fix them.   no   sometimes   often

44. I ask myself how well I am learning English,
    and I try to think of <u>better</u> ways to learn.   no   sometimes   often

45. I try to understand the Australian way of life.   no   sometimes   often

Appendix 5: Guidelines for observation by student teachers

A. Introduction
1. Teachers are busy professionals. Classroom observations are not always a welcome intrusion for the classroom teachers involved.
2. The observation of classroom teachers is serious business; it should not be approached casually.
3. Learning how to observe in a manner acceptable to all parties takes time, careful reflection, personal tact, and creativity.
4. An observer is a guest in the teacher's and the students' classroom. A guest in the classroom is there thanks to the goodwill of the cooperating teacher.
5. A guest's purpose for visiting is not to judge, evaluate, or criticize the classroom teacher, or to offer suggestions, but simply to learn through observing.

B. Procedures
1. Visitors should contact the cooperating teacher for a brief orientation to the class.
2. A visitor who is planning to observe a class should arrive in the classroom a few minutes ahead of time.
3. If something unexpected comes up and the visitor is not able to observe a class at the agreed-upon time, the visitor needs to notify the classroom teacher as soon as possible. It is a visitor's responsibility to keep the classroom teacher informed.
4. Once having entered a classroom, the visitor should try to be as unobtrusive as possible, sitting where directed by the teacher.
5. If a student in the class asks the visitor a direct question (e.g., What are you doing here? Are you a teacher too?), the visitor should answer as briefly as possible. It is important to bear in mind that the visitor is not a regular member of the class. Visitors should not initiate or pursue conversations unnecessarily.
6. A visitor should be appreciative and polite. At the earliest opportunity, the visitor should thank the classroom teacher for having made possible the opportunity to visit the classroom.
7. A visitor who is taking written notes or collecting information in some other way should do this as unobtrusively as possible. The visitor must make sure that the teacher and students are comfortable with any procedures used for data collection.

C. Post-visitation
  1. It is imperative for the visitor to keep impressions of the class private and confidential.
  2. The visitors should explain to the classroom teacher that the teacher's name will not be used in any discussions with other people. Any direct references to teachers, in either formal or informal settings, will be anonymous.
  3. Any notes or information collected during a classroom visit should be made accessible to the teacher, if he or she requests.

(Adapted from Murphy 1991.)

Appendix 6: Guidelines for peer observation

A. General principles

   1. *Observation should have a focus.* The value of observation is increased if the observer knows what to look for. An observation that concludes with a comment such as, "Oh, that was a really nice lesson," is not particularly helpful to either party. On the other hand, giving the observer a task, such as collecting information on student participation patterns during a lesson, provides a focus for the observer and collects useful information for the teacher.

   2. *Observers should use specific procedures.* Lessons are complex events with many different activities occurring simultaneously. If the observer wants to observe teacher-student interaction, for example, a variety of procedures could be used to make this task more effective.

   3. *The observer should remain an observer.* An observer who is also a participant in the lesson cannot observe effectively.

B. Suggested procedures

   1. *Arrange a pre-observation orientation session.* Before beginning the observations, the two teachers meet to discuss the nature of the class observed, the kind of material being taught, the teacher's approach to teaching, the kinds of students in the class, typical patterns of interaction and class participation, and so on.

   2. *Identify a focus for the observation.* For example:

     • Organization of the lesson: the entry, structuring, and closure of the lesson.

     • Teacher's time management: allotment of time to different activities during the lesson.

     • Students' performance on tasks: the strategies, procedures, and interaction patterns employed by students in completing a task.

- Time-on-task: the extent to which students were actively engaged during a task.

- Teacher questions and student responses: the types of questions teachers asked during a lesson and the way students responded.

- Students' performance during pair work: the way students completed a pair work task, the responses they made during the task, and the type of language they used.

- Classroom interaction: teacher-student and student-student interaction patterns during a lesson.

- Group work: students' use of L1 versus L2 during group work, students' time-on-task during group work, and the dynamics of group activities.

3. *Develop procedures for the observer to use.* For example:

- Timed samples: the observer notes down specific behavior displayed at specified time intervals during a lesson.

- Coding forms: the observer checks the appropriate category on a set of coded categories of classroom behaviors whenever a behavior is displayed during the lesson.

- Descriptive narrative (broad): the observer writes a narrative summarizing the main events that occur during the lesson.

- Descriptive narrative (narrow): the observer writes a narrative focusing on a particular aspect of a lesson. For example, the observer describes what a single student did and said throughout the lesson.

4. *Carry out the observation.* The observer visits his or her partner's class and completes the observation, using the procedures that both parties have agreed on.

5. *Arrange a post-observation session.* The two teachers meet as soon as possible after the lesson. The observer reports on

the information collected during the lesson and discusses it with the teacher.

(Based on Richards and Lockhart 1991–1992, pp. 7–10.)

Appendix 7: Guidelines for conducting action research

INITIAL REFLECTION

To start an action research project, you need to decide on a theme. A theme may start at the level of a general concern, a perceived need, or a problem with a class you are teaching. For example:

1. The students in my speech class seem to have great difficulty when I ask them to do oral presentations.
2. When students write compositions, they make little use of the revision strategies I have presented.
3. The answers students give on examinations in my literature class are mostly reproductions of my lecture notes – there is little evidence of any reading.

For these concerns to become the focus of action research, you need to make each concern more concrete, so that it becomes susceptible to change or improvement. You need to devise a specific course of action, which you can try out to see if it affects your original concern. More specific questions for the preceding concerns might be:

1. What changes could be made to the speech curriculum to give students the prerequisite skills that are needed for oral presentations?
2. Are there any different teaching techniques that would better prepare students for using revision strategies in writing?
3. How can the examination questions be changed so that reading is encouraged?

Some preliminary observation and critical reflection is usually needed to convert a broad concern to an action theme. A concern does not often directly suggest the remedy: educational problems are not that simple. The changes you might make will often fall into one of three categories:

Changes to the syllabus or curriculum
Modifications to your teaching techniques or adoption of a new method
Changes to the nature of the assessment

In action research you are promoting change. To report the effects of the change you need a record of the situation before and after the change. What were the observations which promoted your concern? What are the current practices and the current situation? Some observation techniques can be used before and after a change takes place to examine the effect of the change.

PLANNING

The most important outcome of the planning phase is a detailed plan of the action you intend to take or the change you intend to make. Who is going to do what, and by when? What are the alterations to the curriculum? How do you intend to implement your revised teaching strategies? Try to work out whether your plans are practical and how others will react. You also need to make plans for observation or monitoring your changes. Prepare any questionnaires or other information-gathering instruments you will use.

ACTION

In carrying out your plan, things will rarely go precisely as expected. Do not be afraid to make minor deviations from your plan in light of experience and feedback. Make sure that you record any deviations from your plan, and the reason you made them.

OBSERVATION

The detailed observation, monitoring, and recording enables you to report your findings to others. Those involved in action research should also keep a detailed diary or journal.

REFLECTION

At the end of an action cycle you should reflect critically on what has happened. How effective were your changes? What have you learned? What are the barriers to change? How can you improve the changes you are trying to make? The answer to the last question or two will usually lead you to a further cycle.

(Adapted from Kember and Kelly 1992.)

2 Exploring teachers' beliefs

Teaching is a complex process which can be conceptualized in a number of different ways. Traditionally, language teaching has been described in terms of what teachers do: that is, in terms of the actions and behaviors which teachers carry out in the classroom and the effects of these on learners. No matter what kind of class a teacher teaches, he or she is typically confronted with the following kinds of tasks:

selecting learning activities
preparing students for new learning
presenting learning activities
asking questions
conducting drills
checking students' understanding
providing opportunities for practice of new items
monitoring students' learning
giving feedback on student learning
reviewing and reteaching when necessary

In trying to understand how teachers deal with these dimensions of teaching, it is necessary to examine the beliefs and thinking processes which underlie teachers' classroom actions. This view of teaching involves a cognitive, an affective, and a behavioral dimension (Clark and Peterson 1986; Lynch 1989). It is based on the assumption that what teachers do is a reflection of what they know and believe, and that teacher knowledge and "teacher thinking" provide the underlying framework or schema which guides the teacher's classroom actions (see Chapter 4).

Looking from a teacher-thinking perspective at teaching and learning, one is not so much striving for the disclosure of *the* effective teacher, but for the explanation and understanding of teaching processes as they are. After all, it is the teacher's subjective school-related knowledge which determines for the most part what happens in the classroom; whether the teacher can articulate

29

his/her knowledge or not. Instead of reducing the complexities of teacher-learning situations into a few manageable research variables, one tries to find out how teachers cope with these complexities.   (Halkes and Olson 1984: 1)

In this chapter, the nature of teachers' belief systems is examined.

The source of teachers' beliefs

Teachers' belief systems are founded on the goals, values, and beliefs teachers hold in relation to the content and process of teaching, and their understanding of the systems in which they work and their roles within it. These beliefs and values serve as the background to much of the teachers' decision making and action, and hence constitute what has been termed the "culture of teaching."

Teaching cultures are embodied in the work-related beliefs and knowledge teachers share – beliefs about appropriate ways of acting on the job and rewarding aspects of teaching, and knowledge that enables teachers to do their work.   (Feiman-Nemser and Floden 1986: 508)

The study of teacher-thinking addresses questions such as the following:

- What do teachers believe about teaching and learning?
- How is their knowledge organized?
- What are the sources of teachers' beliefs?
- How do teachers' beliefs influence their teaching?

Teachers' belief systems are built up gradually over time and consist of both subjective and objective dimensions. Some may be fairly simple – for example, the opinion that grammar errors should be corrected immediately. Others may be more complex – for example, the belief that learning is more effective when it involves collaboration rather than competition. Research on teachers' belief systems suggests that they are derived from a number of different sources (Kindsvatter, Willen, and Ishler 1988).

1. *Their own experience as language learners.* All teachers were once students, and their beliefs about teaching are often a reflection of how they themselves were taught. For example, one teacher reports, "I remember when I was a student and I wanted to learn new vocabulary, it always helped to write down the words." Lortie (1975) refers to this as the "apprenticeship of observation." Kennedy (1990: 4), in a report for

the U.S. National Center for Research on Teacher Education, describes this apprenticeship as follows:

By the time we receive our bachelor's degree, we have observed teachers and participated in their work for up to 3,060 days. In contrast, teacher preparation programs [at the master's level] usually require [about] 75 days of classroom experience. What could possibly happen during these 75 days to significantly alter the practices learned during the preceding 3,060 days?

2. *Experience of what works best.* For many teachers experience is the primary source of beliefs about teaching. A teacher may have found that some teaching strategies work well and some do not. For example, a teacher comments, "I find that when checking answers in a whole-class situation, students respond better if given the opportunity to first review their answers with a partner."

3. *Established practice.* Within a school, an institution, or a school district, certain teaching styles and practices may be preferred. A high school teacher reports, "In our school, we do a lot of small group learning. We're encouraged not to stand in front of the class and teach whenever it can be avoided."

4. *Personality factors.* Some teachers have a personal preference for a particular teaching pattern, arrangement, or activity because it matches their personality. An extroverted teacher, for example, reports, "I love to do a lot of drama in my conversation classes, because I'm an outgoing kind of person and it suits the way I teach."

5. *Educationally based or research-based principles.* Teachers may draw on their understanding of a learning principle in psychology, second language acquisition, or education and try to apply it in the classroom. A teacher in a private language institute, for example, reports, "I took a course on cooperative learning recently. I really believe in it and I'm trying to apply it to my teaching." Another teacher at the same institute comments, "I believe that second language acquisition research supports a task-based approach to language teaching."

6. *Principles derived from an approach or method.* Teachers may believe in the effectiveness of a particular approach or method of teaching and consistently try to implement it in the classroom. For example, one teacher comments, "I believe in communicative language teaching. I try to make communicative use of the language the focus of every class I teach." Another teacher reports, "I use the process approach in teaching writing and I make a lot of use of peer feedback rather than teacher feedback in students' writing."

In the remainder of this chapter teachers' beliefs concerning language, learning, teaching, the curriculum, and the teaching profession are examined, as well as links between these beliefs and teachers' classroom practices.

Discussion

1. What foreign languages have you studied or learned? How successful were you? How have your experiences as a language learner affected your beliefs about language learning or teaching?
2. In what ways does your personality influence the way you teach? What are the most important influences on your approach to teaching?
3. Students often hold stereotyped views about English or speakers of English. Is this true of learners you teach or are familiar with? What are some of these views and where do they come from?

Beliefs about English

English represents different things to different people. For some it represents the language of English literature. For others it is the language of the English-speaking world. Some associate it with the language of colonialism. Others see English simply as a means of doing business and making money. Peoples' views of English, or of any language, are influenced by contacts they have had with the language and its speakers. In the case of English, or the language you teach these contacts vary significantly from one individual to another. It is therefore instructive to examine the underlying beliefs teachers hold about English and how these influence attitudes toward teaching it. These beliefs can be clarified by considering questions like these:

- Why do you think English is an important language?
- Do you think English is more difficult to learn than other languages?
- What do you think the most difficult aspects of learning English are (e.g., grammar, vocabulary, pronunciation)?

- Which dialect of English do you think should be taught (e.g., British, American, other)?
- Do you think it is important to speak English with native-like pronunciation?
- How does English sound to you compared to other languages you know?
- What attitudes do you think your learners associate with English?
- Do you think English has any qualities that make it different from other languages?

Although teachers' beliefs about English may sometimes represent stereotypical impressions, these beliefs do nevertheless express realities which may influence classroom practices. In a study of the beliefs of English language teachers in Hong Kong (Richards, Tung, and Ng 1991), English teachers whose first language was Chinese felt that English has more grammar rules than Chinese, although they did not feel English had a larger vocabulary or was more flexible in terms of communication. Hartzell (1988) comments on perceptions of English by Chinese in Taiwan, and observes that English often strikes Chinese learners as being an illogical language. He gives the following as examples (p. 380):

- Noting a large sign in a department store which said "Box Office," a Chinese was very surprised after making his purchases that the girl in charge there said they had no boxes for sale, nor would they have any in the future.
- The clocks in an office had stopped due to an electrical power outage. Some time later, the manager happened to ask a Chinese employee: "What time is it?" The employee glanced at his watch and said: "It's eleven o'watch." He was surprised when told that this was unusual grammar.

Discussion

1. Discuss the questions in this section with a partner or colleague. How similar or different are your answers?
2. Can you add other questions concerning teachers' beliefs about English to the list?
3. The Hong Kong teachers discussed here felt that English has more grammar rules than Chinese. In what ways might this influence their classroom practices?

Beliefs about learning

When learners and teachers meet for the first time, they may bring with them
different expectations concerning not only the learning process in general, but
also concerning what will be learned in a particular course and how it will be
learned.   (Brindley 1984: 95)

Brindley's observation draws attention to the fact that both teachers and
learners bring experience to the classroom that influences their perceptions in subtle ways. Teachers' beliefs about learning may be based on
their training, their teaching experience, or may go back to their own
experience as language learners (Freeman 1992a). These beliefs represent answers to questions such as these:

- How do you define learning?
- What are the best ways to learn a language?
- What kinds of exposure to language best facilitate language
  learning?
- What kinds of students do best in your classes?
- What kinds of learning styles and strategies do you encourage in
  learners?
- What kinds of learning styles and strategies do you discourage in
  learners?
- What roles are students expected to assume in your classroom?

Brindley (1984) points out that teachers who favor a "learner-centered"
view of learning, such as that which underlies many current methodologies in language teaching, would probably describe their assumptions in terms such as the following:

- Learning consists of acquiring organizing principles through encountering
  experience.
- The teacher is a resource person who provides language input for the
  learner to work on.
- Language data is to be found everywhere – in the community and in the
  media as well as in textbooks.
- It is the role of the teacher to assist learners to become self-directed by
  providing access to language data through such activities as active
  listening, role play and interaction with native speakers.
- For learners, learning a language consists of forming hypotheses about the
  language input to which they will be exposed, these hypotheses being
  constantly modified in the direction of the target model.

(p. 97)

Learners, however, may express their assumptions about learning in quite different terms, as is seen in the following comments by learners on a communicatively oriented English class where the teachers encouraged active learner participation and gave little direct feedback or direction to learners.

I just want a program so I know what I have to learn. They're the teachers. They know their job.
There is no system *in these courses. It's all 'bits and pieces'.*
Without the grammar you can't learn the language.
I don't want to clap and sing. I want to learn English.
I want something I can take home and study. We do a lot of speaking but we never see it written down.
You need a teacher to learn English properly – you can't learn it by yourself because there's no-one to correct you.

(Brindley 1984: 96)

The assumptions these learners hold about learning can be stated as:

- Learning consists of acquiring a body of knowledge.
- The teacher has this knowledge and the learner does not.
- It is the role of the teacher to impart this knowledge to the learner through such activities as explanation, writing and example. The learner will be given a program in advance.
- Learning a language consists of learning the structural rules of the language and the vocabulary through such activities as memorisation, reading and writing.

(Brindley 1984: 97)

These differences between teachers' and learners' beliefs reinforce the importance of clarifying to learners the assumptions underlying teachers' classroom practices, or accommodating classroom practices to match them more closely to students' expectations. The consequences of not doing so are likely to be misunderstanding and mistrust on the part of both teachers and learners.

Discussion

1. Choose three of the questions from the beginning of this section and discuss them with a partner or colleague. Are there significant differences in your answers to the questions? If so, how do you account for these differences?

2. Choose a situation you are familiar with (e.g., a country or school district). What assumptions about learning do teachers in this situation commonly hold? How does this influence their classroom practices?

Beliefs about teaching

Teaching is a very personal activity, and it is not surprising that individual teachers bring to teaching very different beliefs and assumptions about what constitutes effective teaching. This can be seen by comparing the following descriptions of how two English teachers conduct their classes in a secondary school in an EFL country.

Teacher A is a female teacher with eight years' teaching experience. She is a quiet, soft-spoken teacher who is always polite and pleasant to her students. Her students do well academically and are always quiet and attentive in class. The students sit in single rows. When the teacher enters the room, students stand up and greet her. They raise their hands when they want to speak, and they stand when they answer the teachers' questions. Teacher A follows the textbook closely in her teaching. She tends to be teacher-centered in her teaching, because she believes her classroom is a place where students come to learn.

Teacher B has three years' teaching experience. His class does not do as well academically as the students in Teacher A's class, although they work hard and are enthusiastic. The teacher has an excellent relationship with his students, but his classroom is much less traditional in its organization. Students do not have to stand up when the teacher enters, or raise their hands to ask a question, or stand up when they answer a question. The classroom atmosphere is very relaxed. Students can volunteer answers when they wish to, so the class is often quite noisy. The teacher often makes use of his own teaching materials, and is often critical of the assigned text.

From the descriptions, we can see that these two teachers above hold quite different theories of teaching. Interviews with the teachers about their teaching yielded quite different answers to the following questions:

- How do you see your role in the classroom? How would this be apparent to a visitor?
- What teaching methods do you try to implement in your classroom?
- What teaching resources do you make use of?

- How would you define effective teaching?
- What is your approach to classroom management?
- What are the qualities of a good teacher?

Both teachers felt that their teaching was normal and effective, although both conducted their teaching in quite different ways. In both cases their classroom practices were closely linked to their views about teaching.

Richards et al. (1991), in their study of teachers' beliefs, found that Hong Kong teachers of English believed their primary role in the classroom was to: (1) provide useful learning experiences, (2) provide a model of correct language use, (3) answer learners' questions, and (4) correct learners' errors. They believed their main role as an English teacher was to (1) help students discover effective approaches to learning, (2) pass on knowledge and skills to their pupils, and (3) adapt teaching approaches to match their students' needs. The kinds of learners they felt did best in their classes were: (1) those who were motivated, (2) those who were active and spoke out, (3) those who were not afraid of making mistakes, and (4) those who could work individually without the teacher's help.

Johnson (1992a) investigated the beliefs that thirty ESL teachers held about second language teaching and found that they had three different approaches: a skills-based approach (which focuses on the discrete skills of listening, speaking, reading, and writing); a rule-based approach (which emphasizes the importance of grammatical rules and a conscious understanding of the language system); and a function-based approach (which focuses on interactive communication and cooperative learning, and the ability to function in "real" social situations). Johnson found that:

ESL teachers with different dominant theoretical orientations provide
strikingly different literacy instruction for non-native speakers of English.
Overall, [the] study supports the notion that ESL teachers teach in accordance
with their theoretical beliefs and that differences in theoretical beliefs may
result in differences in the nature of literacy instruction.   (p. 101)

Discussion

1. Discuss the questions listed in this section with a partner. How similar or different are your beliefs about teaching?
2. Read the accounts of Teacher A's and Teacher B's classrooms again. Is your classroom or the classroom you are observing similar to either of these? How do your beliefs

about teacher student interaction influence what goes on in the classroom?

Beliefs about the program and the curriculum

Any language teaching program reflects both the culture of the institution (i.e., particular ways of thinking and of doing things that are valued in the institution), as well as collective decisions and beliefs of individual teachers. Some programs may have a distinct philosophy, such as the Australian Migrant Education Program, which has been described as aiming to implement the following beliefs about curriculum processes:

decentralised curriculum planning
a needs-based curriculum
a range of teaching methodologies
learner-based classrooms
autonomous learning
authentic materials
multiculturalism

(Butler and Bartlett 1986)

Teachers themselves also have specific beliefs about the programs they work in, as is seen in the following statements:

We used to be very grammar based in my school, but we went heavily communicative about five years ago.
We are totally committed to implementing a process-based approach in all our writing classes.
Our program director believes in learner autonomy and learner choice. Students work out their own programs in consultation with the teachers.

Within a program or school, teachers' views on such things as lesson planning, the use of objectives, and assessment may lead to quite different classroom practices. Some teachers make significant use of published textbooks and "teach to the book," letting the textbook make many of their instructional decisions. Others regard textbooks as a hindrance to their creativity and prefer to make more use of authentic materials or teacher-generated materials. Research on the role of commercial reading materials (Shannon 1987) has found that reading teachers often assume that commercial materials can teach reading. They believe that such materials incorporate scientific principles and state-of-the-art instructional practice. They may consequently become "deskilled" through their overdependence on materials; that is, their input to the instructional program gradually becomes limited to making decisions about presentation, timing, and the orchestration of practice activities.

Teachers also have specific beliefs about problems with the programs they work in, which they may pass on to new teachers who enter the program. For example, teachers in one institution described the major problems in their program:

Teachers tend to work in isolation from each other.
Teachers don't have much understanding of the overall philosophy of the program.
There is no proper way of placing students into the most appropriate classes.
There are too few teachers' meetings.
The assessment instruments we are required to use do not match the communicative approach we are trying to implement.

Central questions concerning teachers' beliefs about the programs they work in hence include:

- What do you think are the most important elements in an effective language teaching program?
- What do you think the role of textbooks and teaching materials in a language program should be?
- How useful do you think instructional objectives are in teaching?
- How do you decide what you will teach?
- To what extent is your teaching based on your students' needs?
- What is your attitude toward assessment in a language program?
- What changes would you like to see in your program?

Discussion

1. Compare your answers to the preceding questions with those of a partner or colleague. How similar are your answers? If you are not teaching your own class, answer the questions with reference to a program you are familiar with.
2. Consider your answers to one or two questions on the list. In what ways have your answers to the questions changed over time? What was the cause of the change?
3. Use these questions or a similar set of questions to interview two teachers in the same language program. Do their answers differ significantly? How do their answers influence their classroom teaching?

Beliefs about language teaching as a profession

Professionalism is a recurring concern of language teachers and language teaching organizations (Pennington 1991). Language teaching is not universally regarded as a profession – that is, as having unique characteristics, as requiring specialized skills and training, as being a lifelong and valued career choice, and as offering a high level of job satisfaction. The degree to which individual teachers have a sense of professionalism about their work depends upon their own working conditions, their personal goals and attitudes, and the career prospects available to language teachers in their community. In the survey by Richards et al. (1991), English language teachers reported their belief that language teaching is a profession and that teachers engaged in it are professionals. They reported that they are willing to assume professional responsibilities, that they can take charge of their teaching, and that they can improve the learning outcomes of their students. They shared a common view toward the language they teach, stressing its value and importance in their community for education, career, and business communications.

Connell (1985) presents case studies of teachers in Australia in a variety of educational settings and notes quite different responses to beliefs about professionalism.

Angus sees himself as a conserver of traditions. But he also sees himself as a professional, and has a well-articulated view that teaching should be seen as a profession. He waxes bitter about its lack of public recognition – 'I think teaching is still a most despised and rejected profession' – and blames 'irresponsible' teachers in the private schools, as well as the activities of the state teachers' union, for this.   (p. 41)

Other teachers do not think of teaching as a profession at all.

Terry . . . insists it is a job, not a calling, with fixed limits of time and emotional involvement. That does not stop him from feeling a strong sense of solidarity with other teachers, and being a firm supporter of the teachers' union. At this end of the spectrum, the image of teaching is rather more like a skilled trade than a learned profession.   (p. 176)

Bartlett (1987) sees the key to professionalism in teaching as centering on giving teachers the means to better understand their own classroom practices.

I think we should be thinking about the best means or best professional development practices that will make teachers *professionals*. We need to find the best ways for helping them to explore their practice. . . . that practice involves exploring the relationship between the individual teacher's thinking and acting within the four walls of the classroom *and* the relationship between what the teacher does in the classroom and how this reproduces and/ or transforms values and social ideals in society.   (p. 148)

Lewis (1989) argues that greater attention to accountability is needed to support language teachers' claim to professionalism.

Teachers of ESOL are accountable not only to their clients but also to the taxpayer, so it is important that they can support their claim of professionalism and effectiveness with systematic evidence of student achievement and curricular planning that is logical and coherent and meets the needs of the client group.   (p. 63)

Teachers' beliefs about professionalism can be explored through questions such as the following:

- How would you characterize English teaching (or the language you teach) as a profession?
- What changes do you think are necessary in the language teaching profession?
- What kind of training do you think language teachers need?
- What kinds of professional development activities best support teaching?
- What kind of support for professional development is available at a school you are familiar with?
- What is the most rewarding aspect of teaching for you?
- Do you think language teachers should be evaluated throughout their careers? If so, what form should this evaluation take?

Discussion

1. Discuss the preceding questions with a colleague.
2. To what extent does the program you work in or a program you are familiar with support the notion of teachers as professionals?
3. Imagine that you have been asked to develop a questionnaire which will be used to investigate teachers' beliefs about some aspect of a language program (e.g., their views about the best methodology to employ, their views about program structure and management). What questions would you include?

Follow-up activities

Journal activities

1. Describe your assumptions about the way you teach or plan to teach in the future. How would you describe these to a colleague? Then review the sources for personal belief systems on pages 30–31. Describe the main factors that have influenced your belief system.
2. How would you deal with the following situations if you experienced them in your classroom? What aspects of your belief system influenced your response?
   a. Students use their native tongue too often when completing a pair work task.
   b. A group of students at the back of the class pays very little attention during your lessons.

Lesson report tasks

1. Appendix 1 is a self-report form developed by Pak (1986). It is designed to monitor student-student interaction during a lesson. Complete this form (or a modified version of it) after teaching four or five lessons on different occasions. Does a particular pattern of student-student interaction occur in your class? Does this pattern reflect your beliefs about the role of the students in the class?
2. If you are teaching a grammar class, complete the self-report form given in Chapter 1, Appendix 3, for a number of different lessons. Use the information in your self-report form to write in your journal about your approach to the teaching of grammar.

Investigation tasks

Administer the beliefs inventories in Appendixes 2 and 3 to a group of ESL teachers. The one in Appendix 2 is designed to help identify the teachers' assumptions about teaching and whether they follow a skills-based approach (questions 4, 6, 10, 12, 14), a rule-based approach (questions 1, 3, 5, 8, 11), or a function-based approach (questions 2, 7, 9, 13, 15). (*Note:* This inventory can be modified for other languages by substituting that language wherever "ESL" appears.)

The inventory in Appendix 3 is designed to identify teachers' beliefs about language learning. Administer it to a group of teachers to determine the degree of similarity in their responses. How are their beliefs likely to translate into classroom practices? (This is adapted from the learners' belief inventory given in Chapter 3.)

Classroom observation task

1. a. Interview a classroom teacher about the method of teaching he or she uses in teaching a particular class. Try to identify the key assumptions about teaching and learning which characterize the teacher's view of his or her method or approach.
   b. Observe one or more of the teacher's lessons and try to identify specific ways in which the teacher deals with the tasks given on the first page of this chapter, which reflect the teacher's belief system.

Peer observation task

Invite a colleague to observe one or more of your lessons and to take notes about the following questions.

a. How would you describe the approach to teaching I am using?
b. How would you describe my role in the classroom?
c. What roles do my learners have in my classroom?

After the lesson, examine the information your colleague has collected. To what extent does it correspond to your own beliefs about yourself as a teacher?

Appendix 1: Self-report form on student-student interaction

Student-student interaction

1. (a) How were the students actively involved in the lesson? Through

   role play (all participating) ☐

   prediction exercises ☐

   gathering/reporting information ☐

   discussion ☐

   other ☐

   (b) Can you suggest other ways to provide opportunities for the students to use and extend their language?

   ....

   ....

2. (a) What was the purpose of the students' communication with each other (e.g. to share their experiences of the weekend)?

   ....

   ....

   (b) Can you see that a reason is essential for meaningful communication?

   ....

   ....

3. (a) Did you allow students to

   use their own language first by eliciting responses from them before providing them with the language ☐

   and

   share opinions on correct usage? ☐

(Reprinted with permission from J. Pak, 1986, *Find Out How You Teach*, pp. 69–72. Adelaide, Australia: National Curriculum Resource Centre.)

(b) Do you see how this can increase student involvement?

....

....

4. (a) What techniques did you use to check out degree of interest in discussion topics?

....

....

(b) Could you utilise such ideas as a sociogram for this purpose, e.g. mark an imaginary line in the classroom?

0%			100%
25%	50%	75%	

....

- You then call out topics quickly and students go spontaneously to a point on the line reflecting their level of interest or feelings (as directed) on that subject, e.g. football/abortion/the Labor Party.

(c) Can you suggest other ways to check on interest level?

....

....

....

5. (a) How did you help to develop rapport between the students?

"Getting to know you" starters ☐

Your model/example ☐

Encouraging sharing of experiences ☐

Pleasant surroundings (pictures, flowers, radio, etc.) ☐

Other ☐

(b) Can you suggest other ways to establish a sensitive and supportive feeling amongst the students?

....

....

6. (a) Were the students aware of each other's difficulties/errors? How do you know?

....

....

(b) Could you increase this awareness by encouraging supportive student-student correction? How?

....

....

7. (a) How was the furniture arranged?

In rows   ☐

"U" shaped arrangement   ☐

In groups   ☐

Other   ☐

(b) Who decided on this arrangement and why?

....

....

(c) Do you think any other arrangement could increase student-student interaction?

....

....

(d) Could re-arranging furniture for different sections of the lesson be useful?

....

....

8. (a) How did the students work?

Individually ☐

In pairs ☐

In groups ☐

In the whole class ☐

Out of the classroom
(e.g. community tasks, self-directed
learning centre or library in pairs) ☐

(b) Which organisation produced greatest student-student interaction?

....

....

(c) Could any other organisation provide the opportunity for increased interaction?

....

....

9. (a) Did everyone in the class talk/participate
with each other or only with the teacher?
How do you know?

....

....

(b) Could you suggest ways to analyse student participation? For example, using a tape recording you might like to focus on specifics such as

- length of statements given out by students
- frequency of statements
- who made the statements
- complexity of language used
- responses made and to what.

Any other ideas?

....

....

Appendix 2: Teachers' Beliefs Inventory – Approaches to ESL instruction

Directions: Please read all 15 statements. Then select 5 statements that most closely reflect your beliefs about how English as a second language is learned and how English as a second language should be taught.

1. Language can be thought of as a set of grammatical structures which are learned consciously and controlled by the language learner.
2. As long as ESL students understand what they are saying, they are actually learning the language.
3. When ESL students make oral errors, it helps to correct them and later teach a short lesson explaining why they made that mistake.
4. As long as ESL students listen to, practice, and remember the language which native speakers use, they are actually learning the language.
5. ESL students generally need to understand the grammatical rules of English in order to become fluent in the language.
6. When ESL students make oral errors, it usually helps them to provide them with lots of oral practice with the language patterns which seem to cause them difficulty.
7. Language can be thought of as meaningful communication and is learned subconsciously in non-academic, social situations.
8. If ESL students understand some of the basic grammatical rules of the language they can usually create lots of new sentences on their own.
9. Usually it is more important for ESL students to focus on what they are trying to say and not how to say it.
10. If ESL students practice the language patterns of native speakers they can make up new sentences based on those language patterns which they have already practiced.
11. It is important to provide clear, frequent, precise presentations of grammatical structures during English language instruction.
12. Language can be described as a set of behaviors which are mastered through lots of drill and practice with the language patterns of native speakers.
13. When ESL students make oral errors, it is best to ignore them, as long as you can understand what they are trying to say.
14. ESL students usually need to master some of the basic listening and speaking skills before they can begin to read and write.

15. It's not necessary to actually teach ESL students how to speak English, they usually begin speaking English on their own.

(Reprinted with permission from K. Johnson, 1992, "The relationship between teachers' beliefs and practices during literacy instruction for non-native speakers of English," *Journal of Reading Behavior 24: 83–108.)*

Appendix 3: Teachers' Beliefs Inventory – Beliefs about language learning

Read the following statements about language learning. For each statement indicate if you agree or disagree with the statement (1 = strongly agree; 2 = agree; 3 = neutral; 4 = disagree; 5 = strongly disagree). For numbers 22 and 23, circle your answer.

1. It is easier for children than adults to learn a foreign language.
2. Some people have a special ability for learning foreign languages.
3. Some languages are easier to learn than others.
4. People from my country are good at learning foreign languages.
5. It is important to speak English with excellent pronunciation.
6. It is necessary to know about English-speaking cultures in order to speak English.
7. You shouldn't say anything in English until you can say it correctly.
8. It is easier for someone who already speaks a foreign language to learn another one.
9. People who are good at mathematics or science are not good at learning a foreign language.
10. It is best to learn English in an English-speaking country.
11. The most important part of learning a foreign language is learning vocabulary words.
12. It is important to repeat and practice a lot.
13. Women are better than men at learning foreign languages.
14. If beginning students are permitted to make errors in English, it will be difficult for them to speak correctly later on.
15. The most important part of learning a foreign language is learning the grammar.
16. It is easier to speak than understand a foreign language.
17. It is important to practice with cassette tapes.
18. Learning a foreign language is different than learning other academic subjects.
19. People who speak more than one language are very intelligent.
20. Everyone can learn to speak a foreign language.
21. It is easier to read and write English than to speak and understand it.
22. English is: (a) a very difficult language
　　　　　　　(b) a difficult language
　　　　　　　(c) a language of medium difficulty
　　　　　　　(d) an easy language
　　　　　　　(e) a very easy language

23. If someone spent one hour a day learning a language, how long would it take them to speak the language very well?
    (a) less than a year
    (b) 1–2 years
    (c) 3–5 years
    (d) 5–10 years
    (e) you can't learn a language in 1 hour a day

(Adapted from E. Horwitz, "Surveying student beliefs about language learning," in Anita Wenden and Joan Rubin, *Learner Strategies in Language Learning,* (c) 1987, pp. 127–8. Reprinted by permission of Prentice Hall, Englewood Cliffs, New Jersey.)

3 Focus on the learner

Language teaching is often discussed from the point of view of the teacher. Elsewhere in this book, some of the ways in which teachers' beliefs, goals, attitudes, and decisions influence how they approach their teaching are examined (see Chapters 2 and 4). However, while learning is the goal of teaching, it is not necessarily the mirror image of teaching. Learners, too, bring to learning their own beliefs, goals, attitudes, and decisions, which in turn influence how they approach their learning. This chapter examines some of the contributions learners bring to learning by exploring learners' beliefs about teaching and learning, the influence of cognitive styles, and the role of learner strategies.

Learner belief systems

Many models of second language acquisition attribute a central role to learner beliefs (e.g., Bialystok 1978; Naiman et al. 1978). Learners' beliefs are influenced by the social context of learning and can influence both their attitude toward the language itself as well as toward language learning in general (Tumposky 1991). Learners' belief systems cover a wide range of issues and can influence learners' motivation to learn, their expectations about language learning, their perceptions about what is easy or difficult about a language, as well as the kind of learning strategies they favor.

Beliefs about the nature of English Learners often have very focused perceptions about which aspects of English they find difficult, and about the status of English in comparison to other languages. This is seen in the following statements made by ESL learners in Japan:

English is much more difficult to learn than other languages.
The most difficult part of learning English is learning grammar.
English is the world's most important language.

Comments like these may often represent little more than linguistic "folklore." However, they do have psychological reality for learners and can hence influence how they approach learning English. For example, learners who feel that English grammar is a major obstacle to their learning may favor a grammar-based teaching methodology.

Beliefs about speakers of English Learners often have specific views and attitudes about native speakers of English, based on their contacts with speakers of English or derived from other sources, such as the media. For example:

Americans don't mind if you make mistakes when you speak English.
The British are very poor language learners.
People are very friendly in Australia, so it's easy to meet people and practice speaking in English.

Although these kinds of opinions may amount to little more than stereotyping, they can influence the degree to which students wish to interact with native speakers. The attitudes learners have about native speakers of English may also be influenced by cross-cultural differences in communicative style between English speakers and people from another culture. A Chinese student in Australia, for example, commented, "Australians are always apologising, they apologise to everyone, even their family and close friends and for such small things! To me, it feels distant and unfriendly. I don't think you should have to be so polite to friends" (Brick 1991: 119). These comments reflect cross-cultural differences in norms for the use of speech acts such as apologies or compliments.

Beliefs about the four language skills Learners' beliefs about language may also be reflected in specific assumptions about the nature of listening, speaking, reading, and writing. For example:

You need to know a lot of idioms to be good in speaking English.
The best way to improve listening is by watching television.
It is a waste of time for me to read magazines in English because of the vocabulary.

Differences between teachers' and learners' beliefs can sometimes lead to a mismatch between their assumptions about what is useful to focus on in a language lesson. For example, a teacher may teach a reading lesson with the purpose of developing extensive reading skills, while the students may think of the activity as an opportunity for intensive reading, building up their knowledge of vocabulary and idioms.

Beliefs about teaching   By the time a student completes secondary school, he or she has been exposed to thousands of hours of teaching from a variety of different teachers. As a result the learner may have formed very definite views about what constitutes effective or ineffective teaching. This is reflected in the following statements by language learners.

Teachers should explain grammar rules.
You can't learn very much from other students in groups.
It's useful for the teacher to correct all the mistakes I make in my
   writing.

Differences between learners' and teachers' beliefs can lead to students undervaluing an activity assigned by the teacher. For example, a teacher working with intermediate-level students in a speaking class reported that she included a large number of group and pair work tasks in the course. However, her students gave her poor evaluations for the course. They commented that they could not see the point of such activities because they could not identify the teaching point.

   Learners often have specific expectations as to how teachers teach and what their roles and responsibilities are. For example:

The teacher's responsibility is to provide information.
The teacher should follow the book.
The teacher should always set an example.

Students can often articulate these views in very specific terms, as is illustrated by the following comments from Australian high school students about what they expected from their English teachers.

[A good teacher is] someone who can persuade other people to
express themselves, someone who can, yes, bring out the creativity in
the kids. Because I think probably everyone's got creativity they don't
use, and I think it's how good the teacher is that they can show that
creativity to the person and persuade them to use it.

[Teachers] need patience, that's for sure. I guess they would have to
have a very creative mind and an ability to judge because for a teach-
er to go home and mark 32 pieces of writing is not the thing that most
people would want to do. So they've got to keep an open mind about
it because they can't just say – well that piece of writing it's no good
because . . . it's written in some other form than everybody else's.

. . . the ultimate thing . . . is the ability and the willingness to sit
down and talk to students, because you find some English teachers

(they're in a minority . . .) aren't willing to talk to their students on a level . . . you get people who talk down . . . which is the worst thing possible for the writing of English because you need to be able to discuss things absolutely straight.

(O'Neill and Reid 1985, cited in Biggs and Telfer 1987: 439)

Learners from different cultures may have different beliefs about what constitutes good teaching. For example, an Australian student studying Chinese in China commented:

The trouble with Chinese teachers is that they've never done any real teacher-training courses so they don't know how to teach. All they do is follow the book. They never give us any opportunity to talk. How in the world do they expect us to learn?   (Brick 1991: 153)

This can be compared with the comments of a Chinese student studying in Australia:

Australian teachers are very friendly but they often can't teach very well. I never know where they're going – there's no system and I just get lost. Also, they're often badly trained and don't really have a thorough grasp of their subject.   (Brick 1991: 153)

Beliefs about language learning   Students bring to the classroom very specific assumptions about how to learn a language and about the kinds of activities and approaches they believe to be useful. For example:

The best way to learn a language is to mix with native speakers of the language.
It's not useful to try and remember grammar rules.
You need to practice every day to improve your English.

Language learners might value some language learning strategies which the teacher may try to discourage. For example, students from a culture where rote learning and memorization are widely used may think that these are useful strategies in learning English. However, their teacher may come from a culture where such strategies are not valued and may try to discourage their use by learners.

Beliefs about appropriate classroom behavior   Learners may have views about what constitutes appropriate forms of classroom inter-action and classroom behavior. These beliefs may be culturally based and, at times, at odds with the teacher's beliefs. For example:

It's not polite to ask the teacher a question during class time.

You shouldn't leave the classroom until the teacher has dismissed the class.
It's OK to get up and ask another student to help you when you need to.
It's OK to copy another student's answers for a homework assignment.

The last statement indicates that what might be considered cheating in one culture may have an entirely different value in another.

Beliefs about self   Learners often have specific beliefs about their own abilities as language learners, as is seen in the following statements.

I'm not a good language learner. I can't pick up the language naturally.
Remembering vocabulary is easy for me.
I feel uncomfortable when I have to speak to a native speaker.

Learners' perceptions of their own strengths and weaknesses as language learners can influence the use they make of opportunities available for language learning and the priorities they set for themselves.

Beliefs about goals   Learners may have very different goals for language learning.

I just want to be able to make myself understood.
I'd like to be able to write well in English.
I'm not interested in learning to read, only to speak.

For some learners, a native-like pronunciation may not be considered an important goal, since they will use English mainly to speak with other nonnative speakers of English. For other students, however, acquiring a native-like accent in English may be a high priority.

Since learner beliefs are influenced by the social context of second language learning, there are often cultural differences between the belief systems of learners from different cultural backgrounds. This was found in a study by Tumposky (1991) of beliefs about language learning held by undergraduate college students from the Soviet Union and American undergraduate college students. Tumposky investigated students' beliefs about the following issues:

1. *Foreign language aptitude.* Are some learners more likely to be successful than others, due to their age, gender, first language background?

2. *The difficulty of language learning.* Are all languages equally difficult? How long does it take to learn a foreign language? Are reading and writing easier than speaking and listening?
3. *The nature of language learning.* Is language learning like other types of learning? How important is the learning of grammatical rules? Of vocabulary?
4. *Learning and communication strategies.* How important is the role of error? Is it all right to guess?
5. *Motivations and expectations.* Why are you studying this language? Will it help you get a job?

(p. 53)

Differences between the belief systems of Soviet and American students are seen in their responses to some of the statements in the questionnaire concerning the nature of language learning and communication strategies.

	Agree [%]	*Neutral [%]*	*Disagree [%]*

It is necessary to know about English/Spanish/French-speaking cultures in order to speak English/Spanish/French.

	Agree	Neutral	Disagree
US	58	22	19
USSR	78	20	2

It is best to learn English/Spanish/French in an English/Spanish/French-speaking country.

	Agree	Neutral	Disagree
US	61	22	17
USSR	100	0	0

The most important part of learning a foreign language is learning vocabulary words.

	Agree	Neutral	Disagree
US	42	39	19
USSR	24	41	35

You shouldn't say anything in English/Spanish/French until you can say it correctly.

	Agree	Neutral	Disagree
US	3	11	86
USSR	11	33	55

I feel timid speaking English/Spanish/French with other people.

	Agree	Neutral	Disagree
US	50	14	36
USSR	24	33	43

It is important to practice with cassettes or tapes.

	Agree	Neutral	Disagree
US	58	33	8
USSR	79	19	2

(Tumposky 1991: p. 58–9)

Just as teachers' belief systems influence how they go about teaching, so learners' belief systems influence how they conceptualize learning and the way they interpret learning within the classroom context. This was demonstrated in Bondy's (1990) study of first grade students in a reading class. She found that students had very different understandings of the nature and purpose of reading, and no single set of beliefs about reading was shared by all children. Six different beliefs about reading were held by the students in the class. These guided the way students approached reading during class time and influenced the kind of reading behaviors they used:

1. *Reading is saying words correctly.* For these children, the focus was on saying words aloud. They viewed reading as performance in calling out words.
2. *Reading is schoolwork.* For these children reading was just another obligatory assignment to be completed before moving on to something that they would really like to do. It was not normally something they would like to do on their own.
3. *Reading is a source of status.* That is, it was an activity to be announced and performed in front of others.
4. *Reading is a way to learn things.* For these children reading meant studying, and they chose to read materials that contained information.
5. *Reading is a private pleasure.* These children chose books that had personal meaning for them.
6. *Reading is a social activity.* For these students reading was a shared activity conducted collaboratively in pairs or groups. It was a source of pleasure with friends.

The first three definitions of reading were common among students in lower-ability reading groups, and the second three were expressed almost exclusively by children in higher-ability groups. They reflect a view of reading as "a personally meaningful activity" (Bondy 1990: 35). Bondy also found that teachers unconsciously supported these different views of reading by the way they interacted with students during teaching. For example, although the teacher's approach with all reading groups incorporated all six beliefs, children in the lower groups received a heavier emphasis on word-based experiences. Similarly, instruction with the higher groups emphasized meaning, personalization, and sharing of information. The children "formed definitions of reading as they interpreted classroom reading experiences in light of their previous reading experiences with and understanding of reading" (p. 39).

Discussion

1. For a group of learners you are familiar with, how do some of their beliefs about the eight issues discussed in this section influence their approach to learning English? Can you identify ways in which their beliefs, in your view, (a) support their language learning and (b) hinder their learning?
2. How does the cultural background of learners influence the beliefs about the language learning issues discussed in this section? How should teachers deal with culturally based differences between teachers' and learners' beliefs?
3. What beliefs about reading do you think ESL students (or your foreign language students) have? Draw up a profile of the beliefs of a group of learners you are familiar with through reflecting on your teaching experience or through conversations with the learners. Do all the students in the class hold the same beliefs about reading?

Cognitive styles

Some of the views learners hold about language learning and language teaching can be related to differences of what is referred to as cognitive style or learning style. Cognitive styles have been defined as characteristic cognitive and physiological behaviors that "serve as relatively stable indicators of how learners perceive, interact with, and respond to the learning environment" (Keefe 1979; cited in Willing 1988: 40). Cognitive styles can hence be thought of as predispositions to particular ways of approaching learning and are intimately related to personality types. Differences in people's cognitive styles reflect the different ways people respond to learning situations. For example:

- Some people like to work independently, while others prefer working in a group.
- Some people like to spend a lot of time planning before they complete a task, while others spend little time planning and sort out problems that arise while they are completing a task.
- Some people can focus on only one task at a time, while others seem to be able to do several different tasks at once.
- Some people feel uncomfortable in situations where there is ambiguity or uncertainty, while others are able to handle situations where there is conflicting information and opinions.

- When solving problems, some people are willing to take risks and to make guesses without worrying about the possibility of being wrong, while others try to avoid situations where there is such a risk.
- Some people learn best when they use visual cues and write notes to help them remember, while others learn better through auditory learning, without writing notes.

Knowles (1982) suggests that differences of this kind reflect the cognitive styles of four different types of learners; who are characterized by the following learning styles.

Concrete learning style   Learners with a concrete learning style use active and direct means of taking in and processing information. They are interested in information that has immediate value. They are curious, spontaneous, and willing to take risks. They like variety and a constant change of pace. They dislike routine learning and written work, and prefer verbal or visual experiences. They like to be entertained, and like to be physically involved in learning.

Analytical learning style   Learners with an analytical style are independent, like to solve problems, and enjoy tracking down ideas and developing principles on their own. Such learners prefer a logical, systematic presentation of new learning material with opportunities for learners to follow up on their own. Analytical learners are serious, push themselves hard, and are vulnerable to failure.

Communicative learning style   Learners with a communicative learning style prefer a social approach to learning. They need personal feedback and interaction, and learn well from discussion and group activities. They thrive in a democratically run class.

Authority-oriented learning style   Learners with an authority-oriented style are said to be responsible and dependable. They like and need structure and sequential progression. They relate well to a traditional classroom. They prefer the teacher as an authority figure. They like to have clear instructions and to know exactly what they are doing; they are not comfortable with consensus-building discussion.

A large-scale study of adult ESL students in Australia (Willing 1988: 101) sought to identify how these kinds of differences in cognitive style affected learners' preferences in six different areas:

1. preferences for particular kinds of classroom activities
2. preferences for particular types of teacher behavior
3. preferences for particular grouping arrangements
4. preferences for particular aspects of language which need emphasis
5. preferences for particular sensory modes, such as visual, auditory, or tactile learning
6. preferences for particular modes of learning on one's own outside class.

The students were both interviewed and given a questionnaire to complete about their learning preferences. The ten most frequent preferences were the following:

I like to practise the sounds and pronunciation.	62%
I like the teacher to tell me all my mistakes.	61%
In class, I like to learn by conversations.	55%
I like the teacher to explain *everything* to us.	54%
I like to learn many new words.	47%
I like to learn by talking to friends in English.	48%
I like to learn by watching, and listening to Australians.	39%
I like to learn English words by *hearing* them.	37%
I like to learn English words by *seeing* them.	38%
I like the teacher to help me talk about my interests.	35%

(Willing 1988: 116)

It was found that differences in cognitive styles affected learners' preferences for particular approaches to learning. For example, concrete learners tended to choose the following:

In class, I like to learn by games.
In class, I like to learn by pictures, films, video.
I like to learn English by working in pairs.

Learners with analytical learning styles, however, reported the following preferences:

I like to study grammar.
At home, I like to learn by studying English books.
I like the teacher to let me find my mistakes.

Learners favoring a communicative style preferred the following:

I like to learn by watching, listening to Australians.
I like to learn by talking to friends in English.
At home, I like to learn by watching TV in English.

Authority-oriented learners reported these preferences:

I like the teacher to explain everything to us.
I want to write everything in my notebook.
I like to have my own textbook.

Information of this kind can help indicate whether teachers and learners approach learning in the same way. While it is not necessary to put learners into boxes labeled according to cognitive styles, it is useful to try to identify which approaches to learning they favor and how teaching can accommodate their learning preferences. It is also important to recognize that cognitive styles may reflect cultural factors. Willing, for example, investigated the cognitive style preferences of different ethnic groups and found differences according to the learners' cultural backgrounds. For example, the learning modes most preferred by Chinese learners were:

I like the teacher to explain *everything* to us.	54%
I like the teacher to tell me all my mistakes.	51%
I like to practise the sounds and pronunciation.	50%
I like to learn many new words.	43%
In class, I like to learn by conversations.	43%
I like to learn English words by *doing* something.	43%

(Willing 1988: 131)

For Arabic speakers, however, the most preferred learning modes were:

I like to practise the sounds and pronunciation.	77%
I like the teacher to explain *everything* to us.	77%
I like to study grammar.	65%
I like to learn by talking to friends in English.	56%
I like the teacher to help me talk about my interests.	56%
In class, I like to learn by conversations.	56%

(Willing 1988: 131)

Discussion

1. Do you think the concept of cognitive style is a useful one? In what ways can this concept clarify our understanding of how students learn? In what ways can it hinder it?
2. Have you taken a course in a foreign language or in some other subject recently? If so, think about your own approach to learning and your own cognitive style. To what extent does it match one of the four categories of cognitive style

discussed in this section? Try to characterize your own approach to learning.

Learning strategies

Whereas cognitive styles can be thought of as relatively stable characteristics of learners which affect their general approach to learning, learning strategies are the specific procedures learners use with individual learning tasks. When confronted with a classroom learning task, such as reading a chapter of a book or preparing a written summary of a passage, the learner can choose several different ways of completing the task. Each of these choices or strategies offers particular advantages or disadvantages, and the use of an appropriate learning strategy can enhance success with the learning task. An important aspect of teaching is to promote learners' awareness and control of effective learning strategies and discourage the use of ineffective ones.

Oxford (1990: 8) defines learning strategies as "specific actions taken by the learner to make learning easier, faster, more enjoyable, more self-directed, and more transferable to new situations." She suggests that language learning strategies have the following features (p. 9):

They contribute to the main goal, communicative competence.
They allow learners to become more self-directed.
They expand the role of teachers.
They are problem-oriented.
They are specific actions taken by the learner.
They involve many aspects of the learner, not just the cognitive.
They support learning both directly and indirectly.
They are not always observable.
They are often conscious.
They can be taught.
They are flexible.
They are influenced by a variety of factors.

There is a great amount of ongoing research into the nature of learning strategies and into identifying learning strategies that are effective for different purposes (Vann and Abraham 1990). Oxford (1990) identifies six general types of learning strategies:

- *Memory strategies,* which help students to store and retrieve information.

- *Cognitive strategies,* which enable learners to understand and produce new language.
- *Compensation strategies,* which allow learners to communicate despite deficiencies in their language knowledge.
- *Metacognitive strategies,* which allow learners to control their own learning through organizing, planning, and evaluating.
- *Affective strategies,* which help learners gain control over their emotions, attitudes, motivations, and values.
- *Social strategies,* which help learners interact with other people.

Oxford gives the following examples of each strategy type.

- Memory strategies
  - Creating mental linkages (for example, placing new words into a context)
  - Applying images and sounds (for example, representing sounds in memory)
  - Reviewing well (for example, structured reviewing)
  - Employing action (for example, using physical response or sensation)
- Cognitive strategies
  - Practicing (for example, using formulas and patterns)
  - Receiving and sending messages (for example, focusing on the main idea of a message)
  - Analyzing and reasoning (for example, analyzing expressions)
  - Creating structure for input and output (for example, taking notes)
- Compensation strategies
  - Guessing intelligently (for example, using nonlinguistic clues to guess meaning)
  - Overcoming limitations in speaking and writing (for example, using a circumlocution or synonym)
- Metacognitive strategies
  - Centering your learning (for example, linking new information with already known material)
  - Arranging and planning your learning (for example, setting goals and objectives)
  - Evaluating your learning (for example, self-monitoring)
- Affective strategies
  - Lowering your anxiety (for example, using music or laughter)
  - Encouraging yourself (for example, rewarding yourself)
  - Taking your emotional temperature (for example, discussing your feelings with someone else)

- Social strategies
  - Asking questions (for example, asking for clarification or verification)
  - Cooperating with others (for example, cooperating with proficient users of the new language)
  - Empathizing with others (for example, developing cultural understanding)

Learner strategy research has focused on studying how learners use strategies such as these and what the differences are between the strategies used by successful and unsuccessful learners (O'Malley and Chamot 1990). Through observing learners as they complete different language learning tasks and through having them introspect about strategies or writing about how they solve particular language learning problems, differences between effective and ineffective strategies can be identified. For example in one study (Hosenfeld 1977), some of the differences between learners with high and low scores on a reading proficiency test were: High scorers tended to keep the meaning of the passage in mind, read in broad phrases, skip unessential words, and guess meanings of unknown words from context; low scorers tended to lose the meaning of sentences as soon as they decoded them, read word by word or in short phrases, rarely skip words, and turn to the glossary when they encountered new words.

Studies of students completing writing tasks have likewise identified differences in the strategies used by skilled and unskilled writers (Heuring 1984; Lapp 1984). For example, before beginning to write, skilled writers tend to spend time thinking about the task and planning how they will approach it; they gather and organize information; and they use note taking, lists, and brainstorming to help generate ideas. On the other hand, unskilled writers tend to spend little time on planning; they may start off confused about the task; and they use few planning and organizing strategies (Richards 1990).

Vann and Abraham (1990) studied the strategies of unsuccessful language learners on a variety of different kinds of tasks and found that what distinguished unsuccessful learners was not the lack of appropriate strategies but the inability to choose the right strategy for the task. The unsuccessful learners in their study

appear to be active strategy-users, but they often failed to apply strategies appropriately to the task at hand. Apparently, they lacked certain necessary higher-order processes, what are often called metacognitive strategies or self-regulatory skills, which would enable them to assess the task and bring to bear the necessary strategies for its completion. (pp. 190–1)

The current interest in learner strategies in second language teaching highlights ways in which teachers and learners can be collaboratively engaged in developing effective approaches to learning. Both are viewed as sharing the task of facilitating learning by finding how learners can learn more effectively. Rubin, one of the pioneers of work in this field, suggests that through better understanding and managing their learning strategies, learners can expect to:

- Gain insights into their own approach to learning.
- Learn to choose strategies appropriate to a task and learning purpose.
- Learn to use these strategies in a classroom, self-study, or job situation.
- Learn to use strategies specific to reading, listening, and conversation.
- Be able to define strategies for improving memory for language learning.
- Learn how to effectively transfer knowledge about language and communication from one language to another.
- Learn to use resources wisely.
- Be able to deal more effectively with errors.

(Rubin 1985)

Discussion

1. Review Oxford's list of learner strategies on pages 64–65. Can you give examples of how some of these strategies can be used in learning different aspects of a second language (e.g., grammar, vocabulary, speaking, listening, reading, writing)?
2. Discuss with one or more colleagues how you typically complete a writing task (e.g., an essay). Do you employ the same strategies? Have you changed the strategies you use over time? Why?
3. Hosenfeld et al. (1981) describe a sequence for teaching reading strategies to high school students learning French: (1) Teach students to think aloud while reading (that is, students describe aloud the strategies they use as they read). (2) Identify students' reading strategies. (3) Help students to understand the concept of "strategy" and to recognize that some strategies are successful, some unsuccessful, and others only "seemingly" successful. (4) Help students to identify strategies that they use to decode native-language texts containing unknown words. (5) Help students to identify strategies that they can use to decode foreign language texts

containing unknown words. (6) Provide instruction/practice/ integration for specific reading strategies. (7) Identify students' reading strategies and compare them to the strategies students used before instruction.

What is the philosophy underlying this approach to strategy training? What are the advantages or disadvantages of this approach?

4. Learners can explore their own learning in a number of ways (Gray 1991) – for example, through:
   a. group discussion (e.g., in which learners discuss their preferences for learning activities or approaches, or how they solve learning problems);
   b. self- and peer evaluation (e.g., in which students evaluate their abilities in a particular skill area and the development of these abilities over time);
   c. peer observation (e.g., in which one student observes another student completing a task, takes notes on how the task is being accomplished, and then discusses it with the peer);
   d. journals (e.g., in which students write about how they solve specific tasks and how they deal with problems which arise).

   Discuss how these activities could be used in a language program to explore the learners' perspective on some of the issues discussed in this chapter.

Follow-up activities

Journal activities

1. Recall your experience in learning a foreign language. How did your beliefs about the following topics influence how you approached learning the language?
   a. your beliefs about language learning;
   b. your beliefs about speakers of the target language;
   c. your beliefs about your language learning goals.
2. How would you characterize the cognitive style you favor in learning a foreign language? How does it influence the kind of activities you prefer?
3. Try to keep a record of effective learning strategies used by learners in your classes or in classes you observe. Do you notice

preferences for particular learning strategies among particular learners? To what extent are your learners adding to their repertoire of
successful learning strategies?

Investigation tasks

1. Design a learner questionnaire designed to investigate learner beliefs about the issues identified in the first section of Chapter 3,
   "Learner Belief Systems," and administer the questionnaire to a
   group of learners.
2. The questionnaire in Appendix 1 (p. 72) is from Horowitz (1987:
   127–8). Adapt it as necessary for a group of learners you are familiar with and administer it. Discuss the findings with other
   colleagues.
3. Complete the learning strategies checklist in Appendix 2 (p. 73)
   and identify the strategies you favor. Then compare the strategies
   with Oxford's classification given on pages 63–64. Where would
   you place each strategy on Oxford's list?
4. The questionnaire in Appendix 3 is designed to elicit learning
   styles and preferences. However, instead of using Knowles's four-
   part system to categorize learning style as described on pages 60–
   61, this questionnaire uses a six-part system. The six categories
   are:
   a. *Visual learners.* These learners respond to new information in a
      visual fashion and prefer visual, pictorial, and graphic represen-
      tations of experiences. They benefit most from reading and
      learn well by seeing words in books, workbooks, and on the
      board. They can often learn on their own with a book, and they
      take notes of lectures to remember the new information.
   b. *Auditory learners.* These learners learn best from oral explana-
      tion and from hearing words spoken. They benefit from
      listening to tapes, teaching other students, and by conversing
      with their classmates and teachers.
   c. *Kinesthetic learners.* Learners of this type learn best when they
      are physically involved in the experience. They remember new
      information when they actively participate in activities, field
      trips, or role plays.
   d. *Tactile learners.* These learners learn best when engaged in
      "hands on" activities. They like to manipulate materials and like
      to build, fix, or make things, or put things together.
   e. *Group learners.* These learners prefer group interaction and

classwork with other students and learn best when working with others. Group interaction helps them to learn and understand new material better.

f. *Individual learners.* Learners of this type prefer to work on their own. They are capable of learning new information by themselves, and they remember the material better if they have learned it alone.

First, answer the questionnaire yourself, and then determine your learning preference by following the instructions given after the questionnaire. Do you have a primary learning style preference? Did the results surprise you? Compare your answers with those of a partner or colleague.

Administer the questionnaire to a group of students you are familiar with. Do the students in this group have a primary learning style preference? Are the preferences for all the students the same?

Classroom observation task

Observe a class and monitor one or two learners throughout a lesson while they carry out a classroom activity. Try to describe the strategies the learner seems to be employing while completing the activity. Compare your observation notes with those made by another person observing the same learner. How similar are your accounts of the strategies the learner seemed to employ? Do you think the learner was using effective learning strategies? If not, how could they be improved?

Peer observation task

Ask a colleague to observe one or more of your classes and note any instances during which you focus on teaching learners to use effective learning strategies. What kind of learning strategies did you encourage? How did you focus learners' attention on learner strategies?

Action research case study #1

Learner strategies

This project was carried out by two teachers in a primary school.[1]

---

1 This case study is adapted from Zornada and Bojanic (1988).

INITIAL REFLECTION

We were interested in learning more about the learning strategies used by our students. We felt that we needed to know more about the strategies used by successful learners in our ESL classes. We also wanted to find out how the learners were responding to our teaching. The following questions were used to guide our investigation.

1. What learning strategies are used by good language learners in our classes?
2. Do our learners use English outside of the classroom?
3. Do they feel good about learning English?

PLANNING

We identified two children, both age seven, who we believed were good language learners. We chose these two learners because they seemed to be learning English more successfully in the class. We decided to collect information on these learners by the following means:

classroom observation
learner journals
interviews

We planned to observe the learners over a term.

ACTION

From classroom observation, we built up examples of our learners doing things such as the following:

listening attentively
asking questions
using the target language both in and outside of the classroom
interacting with others in English
volunteering answers
using resources such as dictionaries

We also interviewed the students to find out what they found easy, enjoyable, interesting, or difficult in particular activities and why. The students also kept journals in which they wrote about their feelings and attitudes toward language learning. They were given the following questions to stimulate their journal writing:

What are some of the things you learned in the lesson?
Are you learning enough language in the classroom?

Are you using the language you learn outside the classroom? Where
are you using it?
Do you look forward to language lessons?
What are some of the things you don't like about language lessons?
How do you remember what you learn?
Who do you practice with?
How much time do you spend on homework?
Do you often do extra homework not assigned by the teacher?
Do you feel you are good at the language you are learning?
Do you sometimes read books in the target language?
Which parts of language learning do you like best and why?
Did you learn anything new this week?
Do you enjoy being tested on your knowledge?
How can you learn more?
Do your parents help and support you with your language learning?

OBSERVATION

In looking over our data, we found that our students used a variety of
strategies to help them become successful language learners. For example, we asked, "How do you remember what you've learned?" Answers
included:

It's easy to remember when you listen.
I do it over and over again.
I practice with friends and family.
I write down things I want to remember.
I stick sentences on my wall in my room.
I spend lots of time going over with my book, because I like it and I
learn. I would still study it if my teacher didn't see it or mark it.

REFLECTION

Even though we didn't learn anything particularly surprising from our
investigation, it was useful to confirm and make explicit some things
which we knew intuitively. We have learned a useful strategy to use in
order to more effectively facilitate our students' learning. The strategy
involves asking the following questions:

How did you go about doing this?
Which way of doing this works best for you?

Appendix 1: Beliefs about language learning inventory: ESL student version

Below are beliefs that some people have about learning foreign languages.
Read each statement and then decide if you:
(1) strongly agree, (2) agree, (3) neither agree nor disagree, (4) disagree (5) strongly disagree.
There are no right or wrong answers. We are simply interested in your opinions. Mark each answer on the special answer sheet. Questions 4 & 15 are slightly different and you should mark them as indicated.
REMEMBER:
(1) strongly agree, (2) agree, (3) neither agree nor disagree, (4) disagree (5) strongly disagree.

1. It is easier for children than adults to learn a foreign language.
2. Some people have a special ability for learning foreign languages.
3. Some languages are easier to learn than others.
4. English is: (a) a very difficult language
               (b) a difficult language
               (c) a language of medium difficulty
               (d) an easy language
               (e) a very easy language.
5. I believe that I will learn to speak English very well.
6. People from my country are good at learning foreign languages.
7. It is important to speak English with an excellent pronunciation.
8. It is necessary to know about English-speaking cultures in order to speak English.
9. You shouldn't say anything in English until you can say it correctly.
10. It is easier for someone who already speaks a foreign language to learn another one.
11. People who are good at mathematics or science are not good at learning a foreign language.
12. It is best to learn English in an English-speaking country.
13. I enjoy practicing English with the Americans.
14. It's OK to guess if you don't know a word in English.
15. If someone spent one hour a day learning a language, how long would it take them to speak the language very well:
               (a) less than a year
               (b) 1-2 years
               (c) 3-5 years
               (d) 5-10 years
               (e) you can't learn a language in 1 hour a day.
16. I have a special ability for learning foreign languages.
17. The most important part of learning a foreign language is learning vocabulary words.
18. It is important to repeat and practice a lot.
19. Women are better than men at learning foreign languages.
20. People in my country feel that it is important to speak English.
21. I feel timid speaking English with other people.
22. If beginning students are permitted to make errors in English, it will be difficult for them to speak correctly later on.
23. The most important part of learning a foreign language is learning the grammar.
24. I would like to learn English so that I can get to know Americans better.
25. It is easier to speak than understand a foreign language.
26. It is important to practice with cassettes or tapes.
27. Learning a foreign language is different than learning other academic subjects.
28. The most important part of learning English is learning how to translate from my native language.
29. If I learn English very well, I will have better opportunities for a good job.
30. People who speak more than one language are very intelligent.
31. I want to learn to speak English well.
32. I would like to have American friends.
33. Everyone can learn to speak a foreign language.
34. It is easier to read and write English than to speak and understand it.

(From E. Horwitz, "Surveying student beliefs about language learning," in Anita Wenden and Joan Rubin, *Learner Strategies in Language Learning,* (c) 1987, pp. 127–8. Reprinted by permission of Prentice Hall, Englewood Cliffs, New Jersey.)

Appendix 2: Learning strategies checklist

A Check-List for Teachers

Imagine that you are living in a non-English-speaking country. (Think of one in particular.) You know that you will be living there for quite some time.... So you will have to 'make a life' there. Given those conditions, look at the following list of basic 'learning strategies'. Which ones do you suppose you would be most likely to use, in your own process of language learning? (Place a tick (✓) beside these.) And − are there some which you would be most unlikely to use? (Put an 'X' beside those.)

1. Comprehending and practising language primarily in real-life context having personal significance: i.e. to a large extent, trusting in 'picking it up'.

2. When listening or reading, directing attention to a specific feature (e.g. a syntax structure: a verb tense, discourse elements, main ideas; etc.): thus, 'selective focusing.'

3. Practising common structures, conversational phrases, polite expressions and other set formulae i.e. learning them off by heart, in order to have a ready stock of conversational gambits.

4. Trying to extend the known by 'hypothesis-testing' (e.g. having learned 'truck-driver,' guessing: what would you call someone who operates a taxi?; but then also, what would you call someone who operates an airplane?).

5. Listening and watching (and deriving meaning from) observed situations, over-heard conversations, etc.

6. Using semantic context, linguistic markers, gestural cues, intonation, situation, etc. to guess meaning i.e. inferencing: allowing outside information as well as inside-the-message clues to fill gaps in comprehension.

7. Interacting with a native speaker, utilizing learning techniques (e.g. asking for repetition, clarification, correction; paraphrasing and asking if that is accurate etc.)

8. Speaking freely, without worrying too much about errors; persevering in a focus on your meaning and getting it across in any way possible: re-stating, giving examples, gesturing etc.

9. Monitoring listener's practical and affective responses to one's productions: paying careful attention to this, and making alterations accordingly.

10. Focusing on understanding meanings socio-culturally: customs, expectations, interpretations, cues, etc.

(continued)

(Reprinted with permission from K. Willing, 1988, *Learning Styles in Adult Migrant Education*, pp. 8–9, Adelaide: Australia: National Curriculum Resource Centre.)

11. Self-monitoring identifying one's own individual difficulties, working out plans for improvement.

12. Comparing, for example, several sentences in an effort to deduce the underlying rule; i.e. in your own way, looking for generalizations or basic principles of language.

13. Seeking from other people, explanations of linguistic, grammatical (etc.) points.

14. Reading grammar explanations, contrasts; doing exercises and drills.

15. Using mnemonic techniques in order to memorize; 'rote' memorization.

16. Making visualizations (diagrams, pictures) to clarify meaning and remember it; or to clarify structures.

17. Using phonetic symbols or some personal system for reminding oneself about particular sound features, intonation patterns etc.

18. Taking notes, writing down new items; keeping vocabulary lists (e.g. by semantic grouping); keeping a personal learning journal etc.

19. Repetition for pure reinforcement or motor practice; for fluency of sound production in stock combinations, phonetic difficult spots etc; pure enjoyment of articulation, sounds in general.

20. Focusing on and learning from public message of all kinds (signs, ads, labels, train announcements, radio, TV, films etc.).

21. Familiarization with a specific language 'field' by deliberate specialization and repeated exposure (e.g. getting to know the language of politics and current affairs by always watching the same TV news program; learning the language of a particular hobby by reading the magazines, joining a club etc.).

22. Working through a 'cassette-course' on the language.

23. Practising the language in deliberately artificial contexts (simulations, games, crosswords etc.).

24. Experimenting with transferring a message from one medium (or format, register etc.) to another: (e.g. recounting, as a narration, the story-line of a movie; discussing, conversationally, an issue originally read about in a magazine or newspaper, or writing a personal letter about the same etc.).

25. Just relaxing and keeping sensory pathways open ('absorbing').

Appendix 3: Perceptual learning style preference questionnaire

Name_____ Student No._____Age_____
Native Country_____Native Language_____
Male____Female_____How long have you studied English ? _____

Directions : People learn in many different ways. For example, some people learn
primarily with their eyes (visual learners) or with their ears
(auditory learners); some people prefer to learn by experience
and / or by " hands – on " tasks (kinesthetic or tactile learners);
some people learn better when they work alone, while others prefer
to learn in groups.

This questionnaire has been designed to help you identify the
way (s) you learn best – – the way (s) you prefer to learn.

Read each statement on the following page. Please respond to the
statements AS THEY APPLY TO YOUR STUDY OF ENGLISH.
Decide whether you agree or disagree with each statement. For
example, if you strongly agree, mark :

STRONGLY AGREE
AGREE
UNDECIDED
DISAGREE
STRONGLY DISAGREE

Please respond to each statement quickly, without too much
thought. Try not to change your responses after you choose them.
Please use a pen to mark your choices.

(continued)

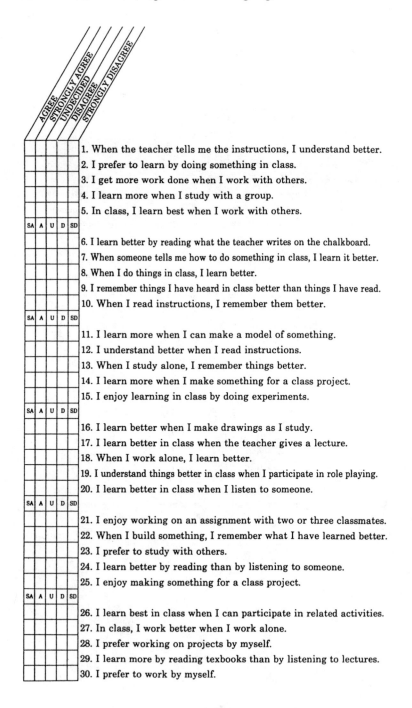

SA	A	U	D	SD	
					1. When the teacher tells me the instructions, I understand better.
					2. I prefer to learn by doing something in class.
					3. I get more work done when I work with others.
					4. I learn more when I study with a group.
					5. In class, I learn best when I work with others.
					6. I learn better by reading what the teacher writes on the chalkboard.
					7. When someone tells me how to do something in class, I learn it better.
					8. When I do things in class, I learn better.
					9. I remember things I have heard in class better than things I have read.
					10. When I read instructions, I remember them better.
					11. I learn more when I can make a model of something.
					12. I understand better when I read instructions.
					13. When I study alone, I remember things better.
					14. I learn more when I make something for a class project.
					15. I enjoy learning in class by doing experiments.
					16. I learn better when I make drawings as I study.
					17. I learn better in class when the teacher gives a lecture.
					18. When I work alone, I learn better.
					19. I understand things better in class when I participate in role playing.
					20. I learn better in class when I listen to someone.
					21. I enjoy working on an assignment with two or three classmates.
					22. When I build something, I remember what I have learned better.
					23. I prefer to study with others.
					24. I learn better by reading than by listening to someone.
					25. I enjoy making something for a class project.
					26. I learn best in class when I can participate in related activities.
					27. In class, I work better when I work alone.
					28. I prefer working on projects by myself.
					29. I learn more by reading texbooks than by listening to lectures.
					30. I prefer to work by myself.

Column headers (diagonal): AGREE, STRONGLY AGREE, UNDECIDED, DISAGREE, STRONGLY DISAGREE

<u>Instructions</u>

There are 5 questions for each learning style category in this questionaire. The questions are grouped below according to each learning style. Each question you answer has a numerical value ：

SA	A	U	D	SD
5	4	3	2	1

fill in the blanks below with the numerical value of each answer. For example, if you answered Strongly Agree (SA) for question 6 (a visual question), write a number 5 (SA) on the blank next to question 6 below.

<u>Visal</u>

6—<u>5</u>

When you have completed all the numerical values for Visual, add the numbers. Multiply the answer by 2, and put the total in the apporpriate blank.

Follow this process for each of the learning style categories. When you are finished, look at the scale at the bottom of the page ： it will help you determine your major learning style preference (s), your minor learning style preference (s), and thoselearning style (s) that are negligible.

If you need help, piease ask your teacher.

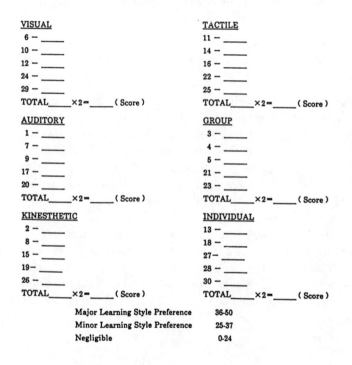

<u>VISUAL</u>

6 – ____
10 – ____
12 – ____
24 – ____
29 – ____
TOTAL____×2＝____ (Score)

<u>AUDITORY</u>

1 – ____
7 – ____
9 – ____
17 – ____
20 – ____
TOTAL____×2＝____ (Score)

<u>KINESTHETIC</u>

2 – ____
8 – ____
15 – ____
19– ____
26 – ____
TOTAL____×2＝____ (Score)

<u>TACTILE</u>

11 – ____
14 – ____
16 – ____
22 – ____
25 – ____
TOTAL____×2＝____ (Score)

<u>GROUP</u>

3 – ____
4 – ____
5 – ____
21 – ____
23 – ____
TOTAL____×2＝____ (Score)

<u>INDIVIDUAL</u>

13 – ____
18 – ____
27– ____
28 – ____
30 – ____
TOTAL____×2＝____ (Score)

Major Learning Style Preference	36-50
Minor Learning Style Preference	25-37
Negligible	0-24

4 Teacher decision making

Chapter 2 examined the role that beliefs play in shaping the instructional decisions and practices that teachers make use of in teaching. This chapter examines the nature of teacher decision making in more detail and the effects of these decisions on teaching and learning. For many educationists, decision making is viewed as an essential teaching competency. Shavelson (1973: 143–5) observed:

Any teaching act is the result of a decision, either conscious or unconscious . . . What distinguishes the exceptional teacher is not the ability to ask, say, a higher-order question, but the ability to decide *when to ask* such a question.

From this perspective, teaching is essentially a thinking process. Teachers are constantly confronted with a range of different options and are required to select from among these options the ones they think are best suited to a particular goal. The option the teacher selects is known as a decision (Kindsvatter, Wilen, and Ishler 1988). Teaching involves making a great number of individual decisions. Before a lesson can be taught it must be planned. Decisions at this stage are called *planning decisions*. During the lesson itself, another level of decision making is involved. The teacher has to make on-the-spot decisions concerning different aspects of the lesson, many of which may not have been planned. These are known as *interactive decisions*. After the lesson, the teacher must make decisions about its effectiveness and what the follow-up to the lesson will be. These are known as *evaluative decisions*. These three types of decisions form the focus of this chapter.

Planning decisions

Teachers differ in the extent to which they plan lessons and in the kind of planning they employ. Some teachers develop "macro-plans," or overall goals for a course or a class, and use these to help them develop the lesson plans they use on a day-to-day basis. In a study of an ESL reading teacher, Richards (1990: 95) found that the teacher used instructional objectives to guide and organize lessons.

> The teacher uses statements of course objectives to help him plan and organize his teaching. For the lesson observed, the teacher was able to formulate what the lesson was intended to accomplish and how its goals were to be achieved. Although the objectives he used were not stated as *behavioral* objectives, they nonetheless served as a way of clarifying and formulating his own intentions and selecting appropriate learning experiences.

Other teachers work more at the "micro-level," planning more on a day-to-day basis without necessarily making regular reference to their course goals or objectives.

In initial teacher training, teachers are generally encouraged to develop lesson plans for every lesson that they teach. The lesson plan is intended to help the teacher organize the lesson efficiently and effectively, and usually includes a description of the aims or objectives of the lesson, the activities students will carry out, the time needed for each activity, teaching aids to be used, teaching strategies to be used, grouping arrangements employed for each activity, possible problems that might be encountered, and alternative possibilities (see Appendix 1).

One school of thought on lesson planning has argued that lesson plans should include a description of intended learning outcomes at the end of the lesson. These are sometimes expressed in terms of behavioral objectives. A behavioral objective has the following dimensions:

> 1) the students as the subject, 2) an action verb that defines behavior or performance to be learned, 3) conditions under which the student will demonstrate what is learned, and 4) minimum level of performance required after instruction.
>
> (Findley and Nathan 1980: 226)

For example, in a grammar lesson the teacher's objectives might include the following:

> Students will be able to write a short paragraph about themselves using verbs in the present tense, including the verbs *live, go, study, like, be,* and *have,* with no more than three mistakes of grammar and spelling.

For a lesson on speaking skills, one objective might be:

Students will practice short conversational exchanges involving greetings and leave taking. They will take part in classroom role-play activities involving social situations and will exchange greetings with other classmates and with the teacher.

Nunan (1988: 61) points out that making course or lesson objectives explicit in this way achieves the following:

Learners come to have a more realistic idea of what can be achieved in a given course.
Learning comes to be seen as the gradual accretion of achievable goals.
Students develop greater sensitivity to their role as language learners and their rather vague notions of what it is to be a learner become much sharper.
Self-evaluation becomes more feasible.
Classroom activities can be seen to relate to learners' real-life needs.
The development of skills can be seen as a gradual rather than an all-or-nothing process.

Brindley (1984), in a study of teachers' use of objectives in a program for adult migrant ESL students, found that teachers tended to state objectives in terms of what the teacher would do and what language content was to be presented, rather than in terms of what learners would do. Brindley classifies the teachers' use of objectives into four categories.

Instructional goals   Many teachers expressed objectives in terms of the teacher's role. Examples of such objectives are:

- To develop learners' confidence in speaking and listening.
- To activate the learners' comprehension of what it is to be a learner.
- To develop learner autonomy.
- To help students become aware of their individual problems and to help them to cope with them.

Descriptions of course and language content   Teachers sometimes expressed course objectives in terms of topics to be covered and activities which would be carried out, for example:

- To concentrate on listening skills.
- To provide input in real, relevant, and realistic English.
- To teach the language of apologizing in English.

- To teach the idea of "going to."
- To give learners practice in using the present perfect.

Quantity of learning content Some teachers described their objectives in terms of how much material they wanted to cover, for example:

- To cover the relevant exercises in the course book.
- To get through most of the textbook.

Learning materials Teachers also expressed objectives in terms of the course book or materials to be used, for example:

- To use taped material from the radio to present students with authentic speech.
- To teach students the sounds of English by using their assigned pronunciation textbook.
- To present an episode of a story from the class reader.

The preceding information confirms the findings of other research on teachers' use of objectives. Teachers do not usually plan their lessons around the kinds of behavioral objectives which they are often taught to use in teacher training programs. Teachers are more likely to plan their lessons as sequences of activities (i.e., the tasks that students will perform in the classroom) or teaching routines (i.e., how teachers present and manage instruction), or will often focus on the needs of particular students (Clark and Yinger 1979; Freeman 1992b). Some teachers report that when they plan a lesson they are likely to visualize a particular class and specific groups of students rather than think in terms of objectives. A teacher teaching listening comprehension to EFL students describes her plan in this way:

Although I do try to articulate objectives, my method of planning still begins with activities [and] visions of the class. It is only when I look at these visions that I can begin to analyze why I am doing what [I'm doing]. I also need to be in dialogue with students so it's hard for me to formulate things in the abstract without some kind of student input. . . . so my planning process is based on layers and layers of assumptions, experiences and knowledge. I have to dig deep down to find out why I make the decisions I do. (Fujiwara, in preparation, cited in Freeman 1992b: 3)

Another teacher describes his approach to planning for a writing class in this way:

First of all I think about where we got up to in our last lesson and the kinds of problems students had with the last writing task I gave them. Then I think of a topic that will motivate them throughout the lesson and which will enable me to work on the students' specific writing problems and build on what we have done previously.

The planning options a teacher employs reflect the teacher's beliefs about teaching and learning. Some teachers believe that lessons should be spontaneous and that a detailed lesson plan restricts the teacher's choices and discourages responding to students' needs and interests. Others feel that without a detailed lesson plan, they might wander off task and not cover the prescribed lesson content. Some teachers work from a written lesson plan with varying degrees of specificity, while others work from a mental lesson plan with nothing written down.

Planning decisions are made after a process of reflection (Neely 1986), during which the teacher has to consider questions such as the following:

- What do I want my students to learn from this lesson?
- Why should I teach this lesson?
- How well do I understand the content of the lesson?
- What activities will be included in the lesson?
- How will the lesson connect to what students already know?
- How much time will I need for each activity?
- How will I organize the lesson into stages or sections?
- How will I begin and conclude the lesson?
- Is the lesson going to be too easy/difficult for this class?
- How will I deal with different student ability levels in the class?
- What attention do I need to give the other students while I'm working with this small group?
- What students have special needs that should be attended to during the lesson?
- How will I check on student understanding?
- What role will I take on during this lesson?
- What discipline and management techniques will I incorporate?
- What grouping arrangements will I use?
- How will I handle interruptions to limit interference in this lesson?
- What are my alternative plans if problems arise with some aspect of the lesson?
- What will I do if I have too little or too much time?

Discussion

1. Discuss with a partner or group of colleagues your approaches to lesson planning or your beliefs about the nature of lesson planning. What kind of planning do you think is necessary? What do you see as the purpose of a lesson plan?
2. If you are teaching a class, write a lesson report of a lesson you teach. Then compare it with your lesson plan. In what ways did you depart from your plan? Why? If you are observing a class, compare the teacher's lesson plan with your lesson report.
3. Interview two or three teachers and find out how they approach lesson planning. Do they prefer using written or mental lesson plans? What reasons do they give for their preference? What do they consider in making their plans? How similar are the approaches they use? What accounts for differences in the way teachers approach lesson planning?
4. The following are examples of behavioral objectives for a basic-level survival skills language course.

   – Given an oral request, the learner will say his/her name, address, and telephone number to a native speaker of English and spell his/her name, street, and city so that an interviewer may write down the data with 100% accuracy.
   – Given oral directions for a 4-step physical action, the learner will follow the directions with 100% accuracy.

   (Findley and Nathan 1980: 226)

   How useful do you think these kinds of objectives are?
5. Examine the guidelines for lesson planning given in Appendix 1. To what extent do you follow such guidelines in planning lessons?

Interactive decisions

Although planning decisions may form the starting point of a lesson, they are not the sole determinant of what happens during a lesson. Lessons are dynamic in nature, to some extent unpredictable, and characterized by constant change. Teachers therefore have to continuously make decisions that are appropriate to the specific dynamics of the lesson they are teaching. These kinds of decisions are called *interactive decisions*. Parker (1984: 220) observes:

Teaching–learning contexts change, and teachers' behaviors must change accordingly. The basic problem for teachers is, therefore, to acknowledge that there is no one best way to behave, and then to learn to make decisions in such ways that their behaviors are continually appropriate to the dynamic, moment-to-moment complexity of the classroom.

The ability to make appropriate interactive decisions is clearly an essential teaching skill, since interactive decisions enable teachers to assess students' response to teaching and to modify their instruction in order to provide optimal support for learning. A teacher whose teaching is guided solely by a lesson plan and who ignores the interactional dynamics of the teaching–learning process is hence less likely to be able to respond to students' needs.

There are a number of components to an interactive decision:

Monitoring one's teaching and evaluating what is happening at a particular point in the lesson.
Recognizing that a number of different courses of action are possible.
Selecting a particular course of action.
Evaluating the consequences of the choice.

The ability to monitor one's own instruction and evaluate it in terms of its appropriateness within a specific and immediate context is central to interactive decision making. It involves observing a lesson as it proceeds and asking questions of the following kind:

- Do the students understand this? Are my instructions clear and understood?
- Do I need to increase student involvement in this activity?
- Is this too difficult for the students?
- Should I try teaching this a different way?
- Is this taking too much time?
- Is this activity going as planned?
- How can I get the students' attention?
- Do students need more information?
- Do I need to improve accuracy on this task?
- Is this relevant to the aims of the lesson?
- Do students have the vocabulary they need in order to do this task?
- Is this teaching students something that they really need to know?
- Am I teaching too much rather than letting the learners work it out for themselves?

In monitoring and evaluating his or her own teaching, the teacher may decide (1) that the lesson is proceeding satisfactorily and let the lesson continue, or (2) that some sort of intervention is necessary in order to respond to a problem that has been identified.

The following examples of interactive decisions are taken from teacher journal accounts of lessons, and describe both the problem the teacher identified and the decision he or she made as a consequence.

In my reading class, after assigning a reading passage I had planned a short group discussion to prepare students for a writing task in response to the reading. However, when students began the group discussion task, I noticed that this generated a great deal of interest and a high degree of individual student participation. So, I decided to extend and develop the group discussion activity and drop the written task which had originally been planned as a major focus of the lesson.

In my listening/speaking class, I had included a dictation in my lesson plan. I had also planned to give students a listening practice of an authentic conversation. But halfway through the lesson I realized the dictation had little to do with developing oral fluency for my students. So I decided to drop the dictation so that I could spend more time with the authentic listening to expose my students to genuine communication.

Yesterday I wanted my students to brainstorm ideas before writing their essays. Originally, I planned to have them work individually, and make a list of ideas on their own. However, after a few minutes I realized students were having trouble thinking of ideas by themselves and were very unproductive. So I stopped the class and asked them if they would rather work in pairs or small groups. The students responded that working in small groups would be much better, and so I asked them to rearrange their chairs into groups.

Johnson (1992b) used videotaped observations of actual classroom instruction to study the types and frequency of interactive decisions made by six pre-service teachers enrolled in an master's TESOL program. She found that decisions made by this group of teachers related to the following aspects of teaching:

Type of decision	*Frequency*
Student motivation & involvement	17%
Students' language skill & ability	8%
Students' affective needs	6%

Student understanding	37%
Subject matter content	8%
Curriculum integration	9%
Instructional management	15%

(Johnson, 1992b: 127)

Woods (1991) points out the relationship between teachers' belief systems and their decision making. He describes a case study of two teachers teaching in the same program in a university ESL course. One teacher (Teacher A) was identified as having a curriculum-based approach (one in which decisions related to the implementation of classroom activities are based primarily on what is pre-planned according to the curriculum). The other (Teacher B) had a student-based approach (one in which decisions are based primarily on factors related to the particular group of students in the classroom at that particular moment). Both teachers were following a set curriculum but made quite different decisions throughout the course.

Teacher A explained and evaluated her decisions throughout in terms of having accomplished the planned curricular content. Her focus in interactive decision making was primarily on whether or not students had understood the material and whether they were adapting to and following her presentation. Teacher B's decisions reflected his attitude about the crucial role student input and student characteristics play in guiding his teaching. His role was to determine students' needs, and use those needs as a basis for deciding what to do and how to carry it out, both in course planning and during in-class decision making. Woods concludes:

For each teacher, there was strong evidence that:
1. the decisions made in planning and carrying out the course were internally consistent, and consistent with deeper underlying assumptions and beliefs about language, learning and teaching; yet
2. each teacher's decisions and beliefs differed dramatically from the other's along a number of specific dimensions.

(Woods 1991: 4)

Discussion

1. What kinds of interactive decisions do you think teachers are required to make during lessons? Make a list of different kinds of decisions, then rank them in order of how crucial they are to the effectiveness of a lesson.

2. Look at the types of interactive decisions from Johnson (1992b) (pages 85–86). Can you add other types of interactive decisions to this classification?
3. What is the relationship between interactive decision making and the quality of teaching? Is it the case that more interactive decisions result in better teaching?
4. After teaching a lesson, think back over the lesson and list the different kinds of interactive decisions you made. How did these decisions affect the lesson? Or if you are observing a lesson, try to identify moments during the lesson where the teacher makes an interactive decision. What decision was made and why? If possible, discuss your list after the lesson with the teacher.
5. Look at the questions on page 84. To what extent do you think about such questions? What other kinds of questions might lead to an interactive decision? What kinds of events during a lesson prompt you to consider questions such as these?

Evaluative decisions

Evaluative decisions are those which a teacher makes after a lesson has been taught. They arise from asking the following kinds of questions about a lesson:

- Was this lesson successful? Why or why not?
- What were the main strengths and weaknesses of the lesson?
- Did the students learn what they were intended to learn?
- What did the students get out of the lesson?
- Did the lesson address the students' needs?
- Was the lesson at an appropriate level of difficulty?
- Were all students involved in the lesson?
- Did the lesson arouse students' interest in the subject matter?
- Did I do sufficient preparation for the lesson?
- Do I need to re-teach any aspect of the lesson?
- What would be a suitable follow-up to the lesson?
- Should I have employed alternative teaching strategies?
- Will I teach the material in the same way next time?

Schemes for training teachers, such as the RSA diploma for overseas teachers of English, typically provide criteria for evaluating lessons. For example, in the RSA diploma for the Teaching of English across the Curriculum in Multilingual Schools, candidates are evaluated both on lesson preparation and lesson execution (see Appendix 2). Such assessment schemes reflect the teaching philosophy underlying the program (e.g., the principles of communicative language teaching).

In evaluating their own teaching, however, teachers typically base their judgments on their own personal belief system about what constitutes good teaching. Woods (1991) found that teachers' evaluative decisions were consistent with their underlying assumptions and beliefs about language learning and teaching. Thus, for example, the teacher following a curriculum-based approach evaluated her lessons in terms of how clearly she explained the material and how well she had accomplished what she had set out to do according to the curriculum. She evaluated the success of activities and students' responses in terms of "taking the teacher 'where she wanted to go' according to the immediate plan for the lesson and for the larger plan provided by the curriculum and the goals set by the institution" (Woods 1991: p. 11). Teacher B, on the other hand, who followed a student-based approach, evaluated his lessons in terms of students' goals and characteristics. For example, at one point he commented, "I've been putting too much emphasis on the material and not as much on the needs of the students" (p. 13).

Richards, Ho, and Giblin (1992) studied the decision making employed by teachers-in-training completing the UCLES/RSA Certificate in Teaching English as a Foreign Language to Adults. In studying the teachers' evaluations of their practice-teaching sessions throughout the 10-week training program, they noticed a movement from an initial concern with the effectiveness of teaching techniques to a more holistic evaluation of teaching, one in which the trainees focused less on the mechanics of their lessons and more on such dimensions as structuring and cohesion and student participation in lessons.

As this movement from an atomistic to a more holistic view of teaching emerges, most of the trainees begin to move from a teacher-based view of their lessons towards a more student focused perspective. This movement is reflected in a shift from less teacher-centered concerns to more student-centered ones as the course progresses. Thus while in earlier sessions the teachers were very conscious of managing the different sections of the lessons, using materials, setting up the presentation practice and production phases of the lesson, in later sessions their attention shifted towards the effects of the lesson on students. (Richards et al. 1992: 22)

The study illustrates that as teachers gain experience in teaching and develop a deeper conceptualization of teaching, the criteria they use for evaluating teaching change to reflect their new assumptions, beliefs, and levels of awareness. Richards et al. (1992) also found that the evaluative decisions the teachers made provided input to planning decisions that they make on subsequent occasions. Hence, planning, interactive, and evaluative decisions are interconnected.

Discussion

1. What criteria do you think would be appropriate to evaluate the effectiveness of your teaching? How do these criteria relate to your belief system?
2. Think about a lesson you have taught or observed recently. How would you answer the questions in this section for that particular lesson? How could your answers to these questions affect planning decisions for the next lesson with this class?
3. If you are teaching a class, before teaching a lesson prepare a list of the main goals you hope to accomplish during the lesson. At the end of the lesson, ask students to take five minutes to write answers to these questions:
   a. What do you think were the main goals of this lesson?
   b. What do you think you learned from this lesson?
   c. What aspects of the lesson did you like most? Why?
   d. What aspects of the lesson did you like least? Why?
   While the students are writing their answers, write answers to questions b, c, and d yourself. Then compare your answers with those of your students. How similar or different are they? How do students identify the goals of a lesson? How do they evaluate the usefulness of a lesson?
   If you are observing a class, with the teacher's permission, answer these questions at the end of the lesson and then compare your answers with those of the teacher.
   a. What do you think were the main goals of this lesson?
   b. What do you think the learners learned from this lesson?
   c. What aspects of the lesson did you like most? Why?
4. Look at the criteria for evaluating lesson plans and lessons in Appendix 2. Would these be suitable to evaluate your own lessons? Why or why not? Prepare a checklist which you think could be used to evaluate your lessons. Then compare it with those prepared by a partner or colleague. How similar are they?

Follow-up activities

Journal activities

1. If you are teaching a class, think about a lesson you taught recently. How did you go about planning that lesson? (For example, did you think about objectives? Did you try to visualize the class and activities? Did you begin with available materials and then think how you could use them?) Describe your approach to planning this lesson in your journal. Do you think this was a typical approach or did it deviate from your usual planning methods?
2. Think about a lesson you have taught or observed recently. What interactive decisions occurred during the lesson? Describe how these decisions reflect your (or the teacher's) belief system.
3. If you are teaching a class, keep a record of the major interactive decisions that you employ in your teaching in the next few weeks. Try to classify these decisions according to the scheme used by Johnson (pages 85–86) or using a scheme of your own. Do you notice any patterns in your decision making? In what ways are your interactive decisions influencing the quality of your teaching?

Recording task

If you are teaching a class, tape-record or videotape one of your lessons. Review the lesson and make notes of any interactive decisions you made. What prompted you to make these decisions? What alternatives did you consider before choosing your course of action? In what way did the decision you made reflect some aspect of your belief system about teaching and learning? Do you feel your decision was the most appropriate one? Why or why not?

If you are observing a class, ask permission to tape-record or video the class. Review the recording and try to identify the main sections of the lesson where an interactive decision was required. What decision was made and why? What other decisions could the teacher have made at each point?

Lesson report task

If you are teaching a class, use the evaluation scheme in Appendix 2, or a scheme of your own, to record your evaluative decisions over one or two weeks. Which aspects of your teaching are you most satisfied with? Which aspects do you wish to improve?

Classroom observation tasks

1. Arrange to observe a lesson in which a teacher teaches from a prepared lesson plan. As you observe the lesson, note examples of where the teacher departs from the lesson plan. After the lesson, talk to the teacher about the information you obtained. What interactive decisions prompted the teacher to depart from the lesson plan?
2. Observe a lesson and try to identify points in the lesson where the teacher makes an interactive decision. Describe the decisions that you think the teacher made and why he or she made them. After the lesson, confirm your analysis with the teacher. Was the teacher aware of making other kinds of interactive decisions? To what extent can the decisions you identified be classified according to the categories used by Johnson on pages 85–86?

Peer observation task

Invite a colleague to observe one of your lessons and to try to identify the main sections of the lesson where interactive decisions occurred. After the lesson, discuss the information your colleague obtained. Did the observer notice points in the lesson where you had to make important interactive decisions? For the decisions your colleague successfully identified, would he or she have made the same decisions?

Action research case study #2

Negotiating course content with learners

This project was carried out by a secondary school teacher in an EFL context.[1]

INITIAL REFLECTION

I was interested in finding out whether my students would use English more if they had more say in what they were learning and how they were learning it. I felt that if students played a larger role in planning the types of activities used during lessons, they would be more motivated and hence use the target language to a greater extent. Since I was interested in

---

1 This case study is adapted from Stanley (1990).

how negotiation of the curriculum affects the use of the target language, I posed a question to guide my action project: Does negotiating the lesson content and structure with students increase their use of the target language?

PLANNING

I first wanted to know what my students wanted to do in their lessons, so I wrote a simple questionnaire for them. I also asked them to suggest activities they would like to do for the next unit of work. The results of the questionnaire showed that games were the most popular type of activity. The students felt that games encouraged them to learn and speak English.

This discovery made me think about how I used games in the classroom. I thought I had been encouraging games during lessons, but what had been happening was that games were used only after the students had completed the set activities. So I planned a variety of games that I could incorporate into my lessons.

ACTION

I used a series of four different activities which were, or resulted in, games. When I implemented these activities in class, I invited a colleague to observe my class and focus on the students' use of the target language. I also collected information using a personal diary, tape recordings, tally sheets, and interviews.

OBSERVATION

From the information collected, it seems that the students were actively involved in speaking English, everyone was participating, and that they enjoyed doing a variety of activities in each lesson. My diary entries also indicated that I was spending more time planning my lessons and thinking about how I could integrate the games into my lessons.

REFLECTION

I feel that the negotiation of activities with my students was successful. The students' use of the target language increased as well as their motivation to learn English. This project confirms my beliefs that (a) students learn best by doing, and (b) students will learn a language successfully if they are able to have some input into what and how they are learning.

Appendix 1: Guidelines for lesson planning

Aim: What is to be taught?

1 Decide on the main teaching point. This may be a new structure (pattern). If so, isolate the *use* (or uses) to be focused on. (See Chapter 5.) Or it may be a particular function expressed by more than one form. (See Chapter 8.) In either case, list the forms that are to be included. Alternatively, you might decide to make your main teaching point the teaching of a particular skill (reading, writing, listening, or some other activity). In this case, there may not be any major new language items to be included, but remember that the lesson should still have some focal point or main aim, and that there should be an attempt to balance the different types of activity included in the lesson. (For suggestions here, see Chapter 2.)

2 Which stage of practice is to be attempted with the patterns isolated above (if patterns are to be part of the main teaching point)? (Controlled, freer, completely free?) This will determine the types of activity to be included. (See Chapter 6 or Chapter 2 here.)

3 Choose a suitable situation or situations for the activities you have in mind. (See Chapter 5.) If the situation is already determined by your textbook, think of ways of setting or introducing this situation.

4 What new *lexical* items (or lexical sets) fit in with this (these) situation(s)? (See Chapter 5.)

5 What *phonological* problems or teaching points should be included? (See Chapter 7.)

Activities: What are you going to do in the lesson?

1 Plan the stages to be followed in introducing and practising your main teaching point(s), bearing in mind what you have decided in 'Aims'.

2 Calculate the timing of these stages. Is there too much for your lesson? Is there time left over?

3 If the former, simplify your aims – make them less ambitious. If the latter, what extra activity could be fitted in? (Do you need a warm-up activity at the beginning? Could you add a brief activity at the end – a song or a game, for example?)

4 At this stage consider: Has your rough plan got a reasonable balance of activities? Different skills (reading, writing, speaking, etc. in the right proportion)? Variations of pace to suit the students' levels of concentration, tiredness at each stage of the lesson? If not, make suitable changes.

5 Finalize your rough plan and the timing of each stage. Write this out.

(*continued*)

Aids: What aids are you going to use?
(See Chapter 3.)

1 Which are likely to be most effective?
2 Are they varied or attractive enough?
3 Are you making full use of them?
4 Do not forget that the blackboard is an aid. Plan your blackboard work in detail.
5 List the aids beside each stage planned so far.

Anticipated difficulties: What could go wrong?

1 Try to guess which errors are mostly likely to occur. Why will these occur? Work out alternative strategies to sort these out. (See Chapter 4.)
2 If you have a 'difficult' class, you should look at Chapter 10 before planning your aims and plan a special lesson for your group.
3 If there are likely to be serious phonological difficulties, work out some strategies for dealing with these briefly or include a suitable phonological practice activity. (See Chapter 7.)
4 Bear in mind that no lesson, however carefully prepared, works out exactly as planned. Flexibility in carrying out a plan is one of the signs of a good teacher. There is a danger in *overplanning* your lesson. To some extent you must rely on your experience and instincts to do the right thing when the unexpected occurs.

Now write out your plan in full, stating the aims at the top. Try to make it brief, clear and easy to follow while you are teaching.

General view: Is the lesson going to be a success?

Finally consider these general questions before committing yourself to teaching the lesson:
1 Are the students going to learn something in this lesson? (One hopes that this coincides with the stated aims above!)
2 Are they going to enjoy the lesson? Is it likely to be fun, varied and satisfying?
3 Does the lesson as a whole have a sense of coherence and purpose?
4 Does the lesson connect up with what went before? Is it building on previous learning?
5 Does the lesson lead the way to useful activities in later lessons? Is it opening up new areas of knowledge and practice?

(From P. Hubbard, H. Jones, B. Thorton, and R. Wheeler, 1983, *A Training Course for TEFL,* pp. 319–321. Reprinted by permission of Oxford University Press.)

Appendix 2: Scheme for evaluating the preparation, execution, and management of lessons

---

SECTION 1　　　　Preparation of the lesson

Using the notes provided by the candidate comment below on his/her
preparation with reference to:

　　　　　　　　　　　　　　　　　S*　　　　　　Comments

a) the relevance to the school
   curriculum and to the social/
   cultural needs of the learners

b) the degree of integration with
   ongoing work

c) the analysis of the learning
   demands of the lesson

d) the learning objectives for
   this lesson

e) the analysis of the English
   language demands of the lesson

f) the linguistic objectives for
   this lesson and their relevance
   to the linguistic level of
   English language competence and
   needs of individual learners/
   groups of learners

g) the appropriateness of the
   selection of materials

h) the appropriateness of
   planning of activities

i) the appropriateness of
   the organisation of the class

j) an overall anti-racist perspective

* Satisfactory　Tick if appropriate and comment.

(continued)

(Reprinted with permission from M. J. Wallace, 1991. *Training Foreign Language
Teachers: A Reflective Approach*, pp.138–9. Published by Cambridge University
Press.)

SECTION 2   Execution and management of the lesson

Comment on the candidate's ability to support the English language development of bilingual learners by providing:

                                                        S*   Comments

a) clear instructions and models
of English language usage

b) effective teacher/pupil interaction

c) effective organisation and
management of the whole class

d) a variety of activities

e) effective materials

f) support for understanding

g) opportunities for learners to
apply their existing skills
and knowledge

h) opportunities for developing
English language use

i) opportunities for peer group
interaction

j) effective monitoring of learning

k) a sensitive environment for
individual learners and their
communicative needs

5 The role of the teacher

There are many factors that influence how teachers approach their work and which particular strategies they employ to achieve their goals. The contexts in which teachers work have an important influence on teaching, since different teaching settings involve teachers in different kinds of roles. For example, in some institutions teachers are fairly autonomous and are free to make decisions concerning course goals, materials, teaching methods, and assessment procedures. In other settings these kinds of decisions are made by a supervisor or program director, and the teacher is seen primarily as someone who carries out decisions that have been made by others. Even in situations where teachers have primary responsibility for how they teach, they may assume very different roles within their own classrooms. Some teachers see their role primarily in managerial and organizational terms. They spend a considerable amount of time planning their lessons, monitoring their teaching, and managing student learning and behavior to ensure that their goals are accomplished. Others see their role more as a facilitator, and believe that the best kind of lesson is one that arises out of the dynamics of the teaching–learning situation. In this chapter we examine the roles teachers carry out in their teaching institutions, the responsibilities that different kinds of roles create for teachers, the roles teachers assume in their own classrooms, and how these roles contribute to the teachers' teaching style.

The nature of roles

A role can be defined as the part taken by a participant in any act of communication (Ellis and McClintock 1990). In some interactions, roles are relatively fixed (e.g., doctor–patient or teacher–student) whereas in others, roles are temporary and open to negotiation. For example, within an office, a group of colleagues may have hierarchical roles (e.g., senior accountant, junior accountant, assistant accountant), whereas in a social situation outside the office context the same colleagues may interact on equal terms. When roles are compared (e.g, parent–child, doctor–patient, pilot–flight attendant), they are seen to have the following characteristics:

- They involve different kinds of work and different levels of responsibility.
- They involve different kinds of relationships and different patterns of interaction and communication.
- They involve different power relationships.

Wright (1987) points out that some roles are defined primarily by the work people do, while others are mainly defined by the kind of interpersonal relationships they imply. While it might be assumed that the role of the teacher is primarily an occupational role, predetermined by the nature of schools and of teaching, teachers interpret their roles in different ways depending on the kinds of schools in which they work, the teaching methods they employ, their individual personalities, and their cultural backgrounds. It is these dimensions of teachers' roles which form the focus of this chapter.

Roles reflecting institutional factors

Different teaching settings (e.g., secondary schools, universities, private language schools) create particular roles for teachers based on the institutional administrative structure, the culture operating in each institution, and its teaching philosophy. The role of a teacher in a "traditional" school is reflected in the following account of how teachers function in a high school.

The school operates strictly on a hierarchy: one principal, several senior teachers, and a large number of regular teachers. The senior teachers make most of the key decisions. The regular teachers do most of the teaching and more or less have to do whatever they are asked to do. Teaching schedules are issued, but there is little monitoring of what teachers actually teach or how they teach it. The students, too, have very little choice over the courses they study. They are streamed into science or arts sections, based on teachers' predictions of student ability and exam results.

Other schools function very differently, as is seen in this account of a teacher's role in a private language institute.

There is no fixed hierarchy within the school. A number of us have to serve as coordinators, but these roles rotate and everyone must do it in turn. Likewise, there are no fixed curriculum or courses which students must follow. Instead, counselors work with the students when they come into the program and we develop courses which are tailor-made for the students' needs. Within the classroom, the content of the course is negotiated between the teacher and the students.

Many teachers would prefer to work in institutions where individual teachers make their own decisions about course goals and syllabus content, and how they should teach and monitor their own classes. For example, a group of secondary school teachers ($N = 30$) in an EFL context reported the following information about their actual and preferred areas of responsibility in their school. The numbers represent averages of the responses.

1. For which of the following tasks do you (a) *actually have primary responsibility* and (b) think you *should* have primary responsability? (0 = no responsibility; 5 = total responsibility)

	Actual	Should have
a. identifying learners' communicative needs	3.64	4.68
b. selecting and grading syllabus content	2.79	4.46
c. grouping learners into different classes or learning arrangements	1.79	3.82
d. selecting/creating materials and learning activities	4.50	4.71
e. monitoring and assessing learner progress	4.36	4.57
f. course evaluation	3.54	4.32

If we compare what teachers actually do, and what they feel they should do, we see that teachers would like to have more responsibilities, especially in the areas of needs identification, selecting and grading content, grouping learners, and course evaluation.

In some institutions, the roles of the teacher have been considerably expanded and include:

Needs analyst. The teacher determines students' individual needs following institutional procedures (e.g., a structured interview) and uses the information obtained for course planning and development.

Curriculum developer. The teacher develops his or her own course plans and syllabuses based on student needs.

Materials developer. The teacher develops his or her own classroom materials, using published textbooks only if he or she chooses to do so.

Counselor. The teacher is encouraged to identify students who are having problems and learning difficulties, and to offer individual counsel to students who need it.

Mentor. The teacher assists less experienced teachers with their professional development.

Team member. Teachers are encouraged to work together as a team rather than to teach in isolation from other teachers in the school, and to take part in cooperative activities such as team teaching.

Researcher. The teacher is encouraged to conduct research related to language learning and teaching, including research in his or her own classroom.

Professional. The teacher is expected to continue with professional development by taking part in workshops and conferences, reading professional journals in the field, and joining professional organizations.

When teachers assume roles such as these, new skills are often required and institutional support may be needed. This has been found in the Australian Adult Migrant Education Program, an example of a large-scale national ESL program based upon the notion of a learner-centered, negotiated curriculum. Curriculum content derives from negotiation and consultation between teachers and students, including

such processes as needs analysis, jointly conducted goal and objective setting exercises by teachers and learners, negotiation of preferred methodology, materials and learning activities, and the sharing of evaluation and self-evaluation procedures.   (Nunan 1988: 36)

In a study of the Australian model, Bartlett and Butler (1985: 112–13) found that teacher assistance was required in the following areas:

Needs assessment skills. The teachers required instruments and procedures for conducting needs analysis.

Course guidelines. Teachers requested a framework to use in developing the curriculum.

Bilingual help in negotiating the curriculum. Bilingual assistance was requested to enable teachers to negotiate the curriculum with their learners.

Continuity in the Programme. To prevent the needs-based model from leading to a fragmented program, some form of program management was requested.

Educational counseling. Because of the range and diversity of student needs, teachers requested the support of educational counselors, people who might themselves be curriculum developers and who could direct students into groups that matched their needs.

Conflict resolution. The concept of a negotiated curriculum sometimes led to instances of conflict which teachers requested help in solving.

Teacher role specifications. Teachers requested clear specifications of their roles.

Discussion

1. How can teachers learn more about their role in the classroom and their learners' expectations of the teacher's role? What can be done to avoid misunderstanding when teachers and learners have different expectations of their role?
2. How many of the roles listed on pages 99–100 do teachers have in an institution you are familiar with?
3. What other roles do teachers have in the institution?
4. How do these roles support or hinder the kind of teaching that the teachers do?
5. What do you think are the ideal roles for teachers to have in an institution? How can the institution support these roles?

Roles reflecting a teaching approach or method

The role of a teacher in the context of classroom teaching and learning may also be influenced by the approach or methodology the teacher is following. While not all teachers see themselves as trying to implement a particular approach or methodology (e.g., Communicative Lan uage Teaching, a Process Writing Approach, a Whole Language Approach), many teachers do describe their teaching in these terms and may have been trained to work within a specific methodology. Implicit in every methodology are particular assumptions about the role of the teacher and about how students should learn. Some teaching methods define very specific roles for teachers and prescribe the kinds of behaviors which teachers should or should not allow in the classroom. For example, the Direct Method, which was one of the first oral-based methods to be used in foreign language teaching, described the teacher's role in very specific terms and proposed the following guidelines for teachers to follow:

Never translate: demonstrate
Never explain: act

Never make a speech: ask questions
Never imitate mistakes: correct
Never speak with single words: use sentences
Never speak too much: make students speak much
Never use the book: use your lesson plan
Never jump around: follow your lesson plan
Never go too fast: keep the pace of the students
Never speak too slowly: speak normally
Never speak too quickly: speak normally
Never speak too loudly: speak normally
Never be impatient: take it easy

(Titone 1968: 100–1)

A more recent model of teaching used in mainstream education, known as Active Teaching (which focuses on the teacher's ability to engage students productively on learning tasks during lessons), sees the management and monitoring of learning as a primary role for teachers. In order to achieve this level of teaching, teachers must:

Communicate clearly by:
  giving accurate directions
  specifying tasks and measurements
  presenting new information by explaining, outlining, summarizing,
    reviewing
Obtain and manage engagement by:
  maintaining task focus
  pacing instruction appropriately
  promoting involvement
  communicating expectations for successful performance
Monitor progress by:
  reviewing work frequently
  adjusting instruction to maximize accuracy
Provide immediate feedback by:
  informing students when they are successful
  giving information about how to achieve success

(Tikunoff 1985a: 135)

Other instructional approaches, such as Cooperative Learning (Kagan 1987; Kessler 1992), attempt to redefine the roles of both teacher and learner through a methodology which relies less on teacher-directed teaching and more on cooperative group work and pair work activities. With Cooperative Learning, the teacher's role is to:

Share the responsibility for managing both interaction and learning
with students.

Structure the learning environment so that students cooperate to obtain
learning goals.

Stimulate interactive language use through group work and collaborative problem solving.

Choose classroom tasks which involve information sharing, cooperative reasoning, opinion sharing, values clarification.

Coordinate group activities.

Provide clarification, feedback, and motivational support.

(Hyland 1991)

Language teaching methods and approaches such as Audiolingualism,
Communicative Language Teaching, and Total Physical Response create
specific roles for both teachers and learners. In Audiolingualism the roles
of the teacher

. . . is central and active; it is a teacher-dominated method. The teacher
models the target language, controls the direction and pace of learning, and
monitors and corrects the learners' performance. The teacher must keep the
learners attentive by varying drills and tasks and choosing relevant situations
to practice structures.   (Richards and Rodgers 1986: 56)

In Communicative Language Teaching, teacher roles are these:

The teacher has two main roles: the first is to facilitate the communication
process between all participants in the classroom, and between these
participants and the various activities and texts. The second role is to act as
an independent participant within the learning–teaching group. The latter role
is closely related to the objectives of the first role and arises from it. These
roles imply a set of secondary roles for the teacher; first, as an organizer of
resources and as a resource himself, second as a guide within the classroom
procedures and activities. . . . A third role for the teacher is that of researcher
and learner, with much to contribute in terms of appropriate knowledge and
abilities, actual and observed experience of the nature of learning and
organizational capacities.   (Breen and Candlin 1980: 99)

The following describes the roles of the teacher in the Total Physical
Response method:

Initially, the teacher is the director of all student behavior. The students are
imitators of her nonverbal model. At some point (usually after ten to twenty
hours of instruction) some students will be "ready to speak." At that point

there will be a role reversal with individual students directing the teacher and the other students.   (Larsen-Freeman 1986: 116)

Within both general education and second language teaching since the 1960s, there has been a movement away from teacher-dominated modes of learning to more learner-centered approaches, which has led to a reexamination of traditional teacher roles. However, even so-called innovative methods still require teachers to carry out particular roles in the classroom in order to facilitate the language acquisition processes the method is designed to activate.

Discussion

1. Do you believe in or try to implement a particular method or teaching approach? If so, what is the role of the teacher for this method or approach?
2. What teacher behaviors does your preferred teaching method or approach encourage or discourage?
3. Compare two teaching methods with which you are familiar. How similar is the role of the teacher in each method?
4. If you are teaching a class, what classroom behaviors would a visitor to your class observe which reflect your teaching approach or method? If you are observing a class, what classroom behaviors reflect the approach or method the teacher is following?

Roles reflecting a personal view of teaching

While many teachers may have been taught to use a specific method or asked to teach within a framework or philosophy established by their institution, the way they teach is often a personal interpretation of what they think works best in a given situation. For many teachers, a teaching approach is something uniquely personal which they develop through experience and apply in different ways according to the demands of specific situations. Teachers create their own roles within the classroom based on their theories of teaching and learning and the kind of classroom interaction they believe best supports these theories. This is seen in the following statements from teachers in which they describe how they see their role.

*I believe every child in my class has got the capacity to learn even if
he or she is not aware of it. I try to encourage each student to
discover what he or she is good at and to help them become
successful at it.*

*I believe students learn best when the classroom atmosphere is
focused and where the bright students are not held back by those who
don't want to work. I arrange the class so that the students who are
likely to be disruptive are in the front of the class and I group the
brighter students together so that they can stimulate each other.*

*I like students to work on things that interest them. I think they work
better in groups because it helps them learn from each other. I don't
like giving tests. I try to find other ways of motivating students.*

*I like to encourage high quality learning in my class. I don't think stu-
dents learn by making mistakes. I insist on students checking any work
before handing it in.*

*I believe the best lesson is a well planned lesson. I find it much easier
to teach when I have a detailed plan to follow. I find that I am more
likely to use the time efficiently in the classroom if I know exactly
what I will do and what I expect students to do during the lesson.*

*I believe students must learn to think for themselves. They need to re-
alize that they can learn as much on their own as they can from me.
I'm there just to facilitate learning. I like to keep my lessons flexible
so that students can have a choice over what they want to learn and
how best to learn it.*

These statements indicate that teachers see their roles in different ways.
These may not necessarily be those assigned to them by their institution,
or linked to a particular method of teaching. Teachers may select such
roles for themselves as:

Planner. The teacher sees planning and structuring of learning activities as fundamental to success in teaching and learning.
Manager. The teacher's role is to organize and manage the classroom
   environment and student behavior in a way that will maximize
   learning.
Quality controller. A central task for the teacher is to maintain the
   quality of language use in the classroom. Correct language use
   should be reinforced and incorrect use discouraged.

Group organizer. The teacher's role is to develop an environment in which students work cooperatively on group tasks.

Facilitator. The teacher's role is to help students discover their own ways of learning and to work independently.

Motivator. The teacher seeks to improve students' confidence and interest in learning and to build a classroom climate that will motivate students.

Empowerer. The teacher tries to take as little control or direction over the lesson as possible and lets the students make decisions about what they want to learn and how they want to learn it.

Team member. The teacher and all the students in the class constitute a team and should interact like members of a team.

These roles often overlap. Furthermores, teachers cannot be all things to all people, and the teacher's role may change during the lesson. For example, in the opening phases of a lesson where the teacher is modeling new language patterns, the teacher may be particularly concerned with planning and quality control. At a later stage of the lesson where students are working independently, the teacher's role may be that of a facilitator. The way in which teachers interpret their roles leads to differences in the way they approach their teaching. It leads to differences in how teachers understand the dynamics of an effective lesson and consequently different patterns of classroom behavior and classroom interaction (see Chapter 7). Teachers' personal view of their role in the classroom thus influences how they respond to the following dimensions of teaching:

Classroom management and organization. How do teachers establish classroom routines, procedures, and rules? What kinds of seating arrangements do they use?

Teacher control. How do teachers maintain an acceptable level of performance in the classroom?

Curriculum, content, and planning. How do teachers approach lesson planning, lesson organization, and structure?

Instructional strategies. What type of teaching approach and classroom activities do teachers prefer?

Motivational techniques. What strategies do teachers use to create classroom climate and motivation?

Assessment philosophy. What type of assessment procedures do teachers use?

A teacher's style of teaching may thus be thought of as resulting from how the teacher interprets his or her role in the classroom, which is linked to the teacher's belief system (see Chapter 2).

Discussion

1. Examine the list of personal teaching roles on pages 105–
   106. What other personal roles do teachers sometimes
   choose for themselves?
2. Examine the six quotes in this section by teachers on how
   they see their role. Match them to the list of teaching roles referred to in question 1.
3. If you are teaching a class, do you think your personal roles
   as a teacher have changed as you have gained experience
   teaching? If so, what prompted these changes?
4. Interview two or three teachers about how they see their roles
   in the classroom. What are the assumptions underlying their
   view of their roles? How would these roles influence the
   classroom dynamics and activities chosen? Discuss your findings with a partner or colleague.

Cultural dimensions of roles

Teaching is an activity which is embedded within a set of culturally
bound assumptions about teachers, teaching, and learners. These assumptions reflect what the teacher's responsibility is believed to be, how
learning is understood, and how students are expected to interact in the
classroom. In some cultures, teaching is viewed as a teacher-controlled
and directed process. For example, the Chinese attitude toward learning
has been summarized in these terms:

Learning involves mastering a body of knowledge, a body of knowledge that
is presented by a teacher in chunks small enough to be relatively easily
digested. Both teachers and learners are concerned with the end product of
learning, that is, they expect that the learner will, at an appropriate time, be
able to reproduce the knowledge in the same form as it was presented to him
by his teacher. (Brick 1991: 154)

This attitude toward learning and teaching may not coincide with that
held by language teachers with a Western education, which focuses more
on individual learner creativity and encourages the teacher to facilitate
learning and encourage independent learning. Western education also
emphasizes inductive approaches more than deductive approaches, as
well as collaborative arrangements such as group work, which encourage
learners to assume some of the responsibilities for their own learning.
Differences in cultural assumptions about teaching and the role of the

teacher can lead to different expectations on both the teacher's and the learners' part, as we see in the following examples.

My students are surprised if I try to get information from them about what they want to study in my class. They feel that I should know what they need to know and that there is no need to ask them.   (American teacher in a U.S. based program for foreign students)

If I read something in a textbook, I assume it must be correct. I wouldn't normally question information about the English language which I read in my textbook. After all, textbook writers are experts in the English language.   (Chinese EFL teacher)

When I present a reading text to the class, the students expect me to go through it word by word and explain every point of vocabulary or grammar. They would be uncomfortable if I left it for them to work it out on their own or ask them just to try to understand the main ideas.   (Egyptian EFL teacher)

If a student doesn't succeed, it is my fault for not presenting the material clearly enough. If a student can't understand something, I must find a way to present it more clearly.   (Taiwanese EFL teacher)

If I do group work or open-ended communicative activities, the students and other colleagues will feel that I'm not really teaching them. They will feel that I didn't have anything really planned for the lesson and that I'm just filling in time.   (Japanese EFL teacher)

I'm expected to be an expert about English and I should be able to answer all my students' questions, otherwise they will think I'm lazy or incompetent.   (EFL teacher in Brazil)

Many of the assumptions that language teachers and learners hold about language learning reflect attitudes derived from their particular cultural background. These attitudes influence the expectations that both parties have about the other. Where these expectations are in conflict, there is a potential for misunderstanding. While these misunderstandings may at times be unavoidable, they can be minimized through a greater awareness of their sources.

Discussion

1. How do cultural factors affect the role of the teacher in a situation you are familiar with? Does this sometimes lead to

misunderstandings when teachers and learners with different cultural backgrounds are involved?
2. Examine the six statements by teachers in this section. What issue is each statement a response to? In what ways does each statement reflect cultural assumptions, and how might these assumptions differ according to one's cultural background?

Follow-up activities

Journal activities

1. In your journal this week, describe how you see your role or roles as a teacher or as a future teacher. Examine these roles in terms of your underlying beliefs and in terms of external factors (e.g., institution, culture). Discuss how these roles influence the kind of teaching you do or would like to do.
2. If you are teaching a class, try to recall how you interacted with your class in your lessons, what kind of role you tried to realize in the teaching, and how successful you were. If you are observing a class, describe how your cooperating teacher addresses the same issues. The following questions may help guide your journal writing:
   a. In what ways am I (or is my cooperating teacher) responsive to learners' needs?
   b. Do I try to encourage learner participation? How?
   c. How do I give learners feedback on their efforts?
   d. What aspects of classroom behavior or interaction do I encourage or discourage?
   e. How do I achieve successful classroom management?

Recording task

Record one of your lessons or a teacher's lesson, and listen to it in order to determine what your role or the teacher's role was in the lesson. Think about the following questions:
   a. Do you feel you (or the teacher) dominated the lesson?
   b. In what ways was student participation encouraged in the lesson?
   c. What role did learners play in the lesson?
   d. How were learners given feedback on their performance?
   e. How were misunderstandings dealt with when they arose?
   f. What were the patterns of communication during the lesson?

g. How were the learners motivated and kept interested in the lesson?
h. From listening to the tape, how would you characterize your (or the teacher's) personal teaching style?

Classroom observation tasks

1. Observe two teachers' classes and note examples of how they accomplish these aspects of the lesson:
   a. Giving directions.
   b. Promoting student involvement in the lesson.
   c. Monitoring student performance.
   d. Providing feedback.
   Do the teachers adopt similar or different ways of dealing with these dimensions of teaching? If there are differences, do these differences reflect different views of teacher roles?
2. Observe a language class and focus on the role of the teacher. How would you characterize the primary roles assumed by the teacher? What behaviors did you observe which indicate these roles?

Peer observation task

If you are teaching a class, ask a colleague to observe your class and focus on the roles you assume during the class. Choose one or more of the roles discussed on pages 105–106 (e.g., Planner, Manager, Quality Controller, Group Organizer, Facilitator, Motivator, Empowerer, Team Member) or other roles of your choice. Your colleague should try to note examples of how you realize these roles in your teaching. Discuss the observation data to see if the perceptions of the observer match your own perceptions of your roles.

Action research case study #3

Renegotiating teacher–learner roles to increase student motivation

This project was carried out by a secondary school teacher in an ESL context.

INITIAL REFLECTION

I teach a class of working-class teenagers who are at an age where they are relatively unmotivated and where some of them create problems with classroom management through rowdiness and unwillingness to do assigned class tasks. They are a class of mixed ability levels. Traditionally, my approach to this kind of class has been to try to keep a very tight control over the class, by giving them lots of work to do and monitoring them as closely as I can to try to keep them as occupied as possible during the class. But I have felt uncomfortable with this approach and decided I would try to see what happened if I changed my role in the classroom and implemented a contract system in which students would negotiate activities to work on. I wanted to find out if this would improve their motivation and reduce classroom management problems.

PLANNING

I decided to develop contracts between myself and each student in the class which would cover aspects of the class text students were most interested in working on (e.g., writing, grammar, reading, listening, speaking) and how they would like to be evaluated on their learning. For the first part of each lesson, I would teach the whole class for fifteen minutes. For the remainder of the lesson, students would work either individually, in pairs, or in groups on the tasks they had selected. I had to develop supplementary tasks for many of them to cover the options they wanted to work on.

ACTION

I introduced the contract system and explained how it would work to the class. I developed a chart which went on one wall to show what students would be working on at different times. Once the system got going it went quite well. Although the class was quite noisy, the students were more focused on their tasks and I was able to move around helping individual students or groups. The students seemed to settle down and spend less time disrupting each other.

OBSERVATION

I think the contract system really increased the students' motivation because students had chosen what they wanted to do, and they saw my role as a kind of facilitator. Most students got good grades on the tasks they had asked to be assessed on. I gave out an evaluation form at the end of the term to ask students what they thought of the contract system. Their evaluation was fairly positive. The students indicated that they liked having a chance to choose what they wanted to do for each lesson and to know in advance what was required.

REFLECTION

I have learned how to deal more effectively with students who I might once have considered to be "problem students." I have also learned that students work better if they have more input into what they learn and how they learn it. However, students still need to be guided in making their choices and managing their time. I found that successful implementation of a contract system required changing my role in the classroom. I prefer my new role of facilitator instead of always acting as a disciplinarian.

6 *The structure of a language lesson*

Lessons are events which are fairly easy to recognize. They take place in a particular setting (e.g., a school or classroom), they normally involve two kinds of participants (the teacher and students), and they normally consist of recognizable kinds of activities (e.g., the teacher lecturing at the front of the class, the teacher posing questions and calling on students to answer them). A lesson is, hence, distinguishable from other kinds of speech events, such as meetings, debates, arguments, or trials.

Like other speech events, however, lessons have a recognizable structure. They begin in a particular way, they proceed through a series of teaching and learning activities, and they reach a conclusion. This pattern of structure or organization is a result of the teacher's attempts to manage the instructional process in a way which will optimize the amount of learning that can take place in the time available. Wong-Fillmore (1985: 23–4) observes:

How classes are organized and how instructional events are structured determine to a large extent the nature of the language that students hear and use in the classroom. . . . Two sets of characteristics appear to distinguish classes that work for language learning from those that do not. The first set relates to the way the classes are structured or are organized for instruction, the second to the way language is used in lessons.

Research on teaching in mainstream classes has found that when teachers structure their lessons effectively, they:

Begin a lesson with a short review of previous, prerequisite learning.
Begin a lesson with a short statement of goals.
Present new material in small steps, with student practice after each step.
Give clear and detailed instructions and explanations.
Provide a high level of active practice for all students.

Ask a large number of questions, check for student understanding, and obtain
   responses from all students.
Guide students during initial practice.
Provide systematic feedback and corrections.
Provide explicit instruction and practice for seatwork exercises and, where
   necessary, monitor students during seatwork.

(Rosenshine and Stevens 1986: 377)

This chapter concerns how lessons are organized into sequences and how
the momentum of a lesson is achieved. This is referred to as *structuring*.
The focus will be on four dimensions of structuring:

Opening. How a lesson begins.
Sequencing. How a lesson is divided into segments and how the
   segments relate to each other.
Pacing. How a sense of movement is achieved within a lesson.
Closure. How a lesson is brought to an end.

Openings

The opening of a lesson consists of the procedures the teacher uses to
focus the students' attention on the learning aims of the lesson. Research
on teaching suggests that the opening, or "entry," of a lesson generally
occupies the first five minutes and can have an important influence on
how much students learn from a lesson (Kindsvatter, Wilen, and Ishler,
1988). In her longitudinal study of limited English proficiency students
in third and fifth grade classrooms in the United States, Wong-Fillmore
(1985: 27) found that effective lessons for language learning were

formal, scheduled lessons with clear boundaries. The beginnings of small-
group lessons were usually marked by an actual change in the physical
location of the students or by some other movement . . . [such as] turning
seats around so students face one another. The beginnings of such events
were often marked by changes in the teacher's voice quality or volume, or in
the teacher's location or posture, these serving to call the group to attention.

Lesson beginnings can serve a variety of purposes. For example, specific
lessons openings can be used to:

Help learners to relate the content of the new lesson to that of the last or
   previous lessons (cognitive contribution).
Assess relevant knowledge (cognitive contribution).

Establish an appropriate "set" in learners: i.e., prepare them for what is to
   follow (cognitive or affective contribution).
Allow "tuning-in" time – which may be especially important in situations
   where learners have come directly from a radically different environment
   (pragmatic contribution).
Reduce the disruption caused by late-arriving students (pragmatic
   contribution).

$$\text{(McGrath, Davies, and Mulphin 1992: 92–3)}$$

The way a lesson opens reflects a number of decisions that a teacher
makes, either consciously or unconsciously. A number of options are
available. For example, a teacher could choose to:

- describe the goals of a lesson.
- state the information or skills the students will learn.
- describe the relationship between the lesson/activities and a real-
  world need.
- describe what students are expected to do in the lesson.
- describe the relationship between the lesson/activities and a forthcoming test or exam.
- begin an activity without any explanation.
- point out links between this lesson and previous lessons.
- state that the activity the students will do is something they will
  enjoy.
- do something in order to capture the students' interest and
  motivation.
- review learning from a previous lesson.
- preview the lesson.

The *purpose* of a lesson beginning will determine the kind of activity or
strategy the teacher uses to begin the lesson (see Appendix 1). Rosenshine and Stevens (1986: 381) point out, for example, that beginning a
lesson with a short review provides additional opportunities to learn
previously taught material and allows the teacher to provide correction or
reteach areas that students are having difficulty with. This can be accomplished by:

- Asking questions about concepts or skills taught in the previous
  lesson.
- Giving a short quiz at the beginning of class on material from previous lessons or homework assignments.
- Having students meet in small groups (two to four students per
  group) to review homework.

- Having students prepare questions about previous lessons or home-work. They can ask questions to each other, or the teacher can ask them to the class.
- Having students prepare a written summary of the previous lesson.
- Having students ask the teacher about problems on homework and having the teacher review, re-teach, or provide additional practice.

In their study of adult classes in EFL and modern languages, McGrath et al. (1992) found that lesson openings are used principally "to establish an appropriate affective framework for learning and, to a lesser extent, to establish an appropriate cognitive framework" (p. 105). They also found that learners are sensitive to the contribution of lesson beginnings.

How do these features of lessons affect language learning? Although there is relatively little research on openings in second language class-rooms (however, see McGrath et al. 1992), Wong-Fillmore (1985) sug-gests that openings and other boundary markers within lessons, such as transitions and closings, help frame the event, giving students an idea of what to expect and how to prepare for it.

The formulaic starters used by the teachers helped to signal when these scheduled events were to begin, so the students knew when they should begin paying attention and what they should be listening for.   (Wong-Fillmore 1985: 28)

The following lesson transcript shows how a teacher deals with a lesson opening in a language arts class for ESL students at secondary level. After greeting the students (Ss) and dealing with noninstructional mat-ters, the teacher (T) begins:

T: The other time we were talking about figures of speech. And we have already in the past talked about three kinds of figures of speech. Does anybody remember those three types? Mary?

S: Personification, simile, and metaphor.

T: Good. Let me write those on the board. Now, can anybody tell me what personification is all about again? Juan?

S: Making a non-living thing act like a person.

T: Yes. OK. Good enough. Now what about simile? . . . OK, Cecilia?

S: Comparing two things by making use of the words "like" or "as."

T: OK. Good. I'll write that on the board. The other one – metaphor. Paul?

S: It's when we make a comparison between two things, but we compare them without using the words "like" or "as."

T: All right. Good. So, it's more direct than a simile. Now, we had a poem a few weeks ago about personification. Do you remember? Can you recall one line from that poem where a non-living thing acts like a human person?

S: "The moon walks the night."

T: Good. "The moon walks the night." Does the moon have feet to walk?

Ss: No.

T: No. So this is a figure of speech. All right. Now, our lesson today has something to do with metaphor. We already did simile and we just slightly touched on metaphor before. Now we're going to see what they have in common. So, by the way, do you have your songs with you?

Ss: Yes.

T: Last week I told you we were going to share songs and this week it's my turn to share with you a song that I like. And I have chosen a song by Simon and Garfunkel.

(The class then listens to the song "I Am a Rock" and discusses the metaphors in the lyrics.)

This teacher has chosen several strategies to begin her lesson. She makes links to a previous lesson, she previews the current lesson, and she uses a song to capture the students' interest and provide further illustrations of metaphor.

Discussion

1. Review the list of strategies for lesson openings on page 115. Which strategies do you (or the teacher you are observing) use most frequently? Do you (or the teacher) use any strategies that are not on this list? For what purposes are these strategies used?

2. Examine the list of purposes for lesson beginnings and the illustrative activities in Appendix 1. Can you add to the list of purposes? Choose one of the purposes on the list. Give other examples of activities that could be used to achieve this purpose.

3. You are teaching an intermediate reading class based on a magazine article about the dangers of boxing as a sport.

Think of a suitable opening for the lesson. Does it match one of the strategies listed on page 115?
4. Read the transcript of the lesson opening on pages 116–117 again. How many of the strategies listed on page 115 does the teacher employ?

Sequencing

Another dimension of structuring in lessons has to do with the format of the lesson itself. Most lessons do not consist of a single activity; rather, the teacher analyzes the overall goals of a lesson and the content to be taught and then plans a sequence of activities to attain those goals. This sequence of sub-activities for a lesson establishes a kind of format or script for the lesson. Experienced teachers often have a mental format in mind when they think of a particular kind of lesson, such as a reading lesson, a composition class, a listening lesson, and so on. This format represents the sequence of activities which make up the lesson.

Wong-Fillmore (1985: 29) points out that in the third and fifth grade reading lessons she observed, a typical lesson format consisted of the teacher:

Presenting new vocabulary items used in the text at hand.
Eliciting discussion on the meanings and uses of the new words and relating them to known words.
Having the group read the words together from the list.
Having the group read the text silently.
Having learners take turns reading the paragraphs in the text.
Discussing the meaning of the text with the students.
Making an assignment for seatwork to be done individually.

In second and foreign language teaching, a number of principles have emerged for determining the internal struct re of lessons. These principles are based on different views of the skills and processes underlying different aspects of second language learning and how learning can be accomplished most effectively. The following are examples of principles of this kind, which are taken from ESL methodology texts of different persuasions:

- Simple activities should come before complex ones.
- Activities involving receptive skills should precede those that involve productive skills.
- Students should study a grammar rule before trying to use it.

- Students should practice using a tense or grammar structure before studying the rule that underlies it.
- Accuracy-focused activities should precede fluency-focused ones.
- There should be a progression within a lesson from mechanical or form-based activities to meaningful-based activities.

Often these principles reflect a specific school of methodology. For example, in Situational Language Teaching (see Richards and Rodgers 1986), lessons often have the following format:

1. *Presentation.* The new structure is introduced and presented.
2. *Controlled practice.* Learners are given intensive practice in the structure, under the teacher's guidance and control.
3. *Free practice.* The students practice using the structure without any control by the teacher.
4. *Checking.* The teacher elicits use of the new structure to check that it has been learned.
5. *Further practice.* The structure is now practiced in new situations, or in combination with other structures.

(Hubbard et al. 1983)

In Communicative Language Teaching, the following sequence of activities is often used (Littlewood 1986):

1. *Pre-communicative activities.* Accuracy-based activities which focus on presentation of structures, functions, and vocabulary.
2. *Communicative activities.* Fluency-based activities which focus on information sharing and information exchange.

Appendix 2 illustrates this sequence in part of a unit titled "Giving Opinions, Agreeing and Disagreeing, Discussing" from a communicative listening/speaking text (Jones and von Baeyer 1983). The unit opens with a conversation that serves to introduce the functions and vocabulary to be practiced in the unit. The next exercise focuses on the functional expressions used in giving opinions. The next two exercises are fluency-based activities which practice giving opinions. This sequence of activities is followed throughout the rest of the unit as additional functions are presented and practiced.

In the teaching of writing according to the Process Approach, the following sequence of activities is often recommended (Proett and Gill 1986).

1. *Pre-writing activities.* Activities designed to generate ideas for writing or focus the writers' attention on a particular topic.

2. *Drafting activities.* Activities in which students produce a draft of their composition, considering audience and purpose.
3. *Revising activities.* Activities in which students focus on rereading, analyzing, editing, and revising their own writing.

Appendix 3 contains an example of this from a textbook on academic writing (Leki 1989). The students are first introduced to techniques for generating ideas and planning essays. The next set of activities helps students to use their ideas to write initial drafts. Later activities focus students on revising and polishing their drafts.

The teaching of reading in ESL is similarly often divided into three stages. For example, Nuttall (1982) lists the following activities within a reading lesson:

1. *Pre-reading activities.* Activities which prepare the students for reading the text. Such activities could include providing a reason for reading, introducing the text, breaking up the text, dealing with new language, and asking signpost questions.
2. *While-reading activities.* Activities which students complete as they read and which may be either individual, group, or whole-class.
3. *Post-reading activities.* Activities which are designed to provide a global understanding of the text in terms of evaluation and personal response. Such activities could include eliciting a personal response from the students, linking the content with the student's own experience, establishing relationships between this text and others, and evaluating characters, incidents, ideas, and arguments.

This sequence is illustrated in Appendix 4, which is from a text on advanced reading skills (Barr, Clegg, and Wallace 1981). Before students read a passage on choosing a place to live, they are led through a series of activities which serve to generate ideas about the topic. They then read the text section by section, completing while-reading activities which involve prediction and information gathering. After reading the text, students complete comprehension and evaluation tasks.

Individual teachers often develop their own formats for lessons, evolving personal variations on the formats they have been trained to use. Wong-Fillmore (1985) points out that experienced teachers are often consistent in how they organize their lessons and in the sequence of sub-activities they use for particular kinds of lessons. While this might appear to be an example of unimaginative, routinized teaching behavior, there are advantages for learners.

Once [the learners] learn the sequence of sub-activities for each subject, they can follow the lesson without having to figure out afresh what is happening each day. They know what they are supposed to do and what they should be getting out of each phase of the lesson; thus they are ahead of the game in figuring out what they are supposed to be learning each day.   (Wong-Fillmore 1985: 29)

In dividing a lesson into sub-activities, the teacher also needs to consider the transitions between one sub-activity and another within a lesson. Research on elementary classrooms suggests that over thirty major transitions occur per day in such classes, accounting for approximately 15% of classroom time (Doyle 1986). In many ESL classrooms, particularly those focusing on communicative activities in pairs or small groups, there is frequent reorganization of learners for different activities, and transition time can be significant.

According to Doyle (1986), skilled teachers mark the onset of transitions clearly, orchestrate transitions actively, and minimize the loss of momentum during these changes in activities. Less effective teachers, on the other hand, tend to blend activities together, fail to monitor events during transitions, and take excessively long to complete the movement between segments of a lesson. Thus effective transitions help maintain students' attention during transition times and establish a link between one activity and the next.

Teachers achieve transitions through cuing and interactional negotiation, which signals the beginning of a change, the reorientation of focus, or the beginning of a new segment. The way in which teachers handle transitions depends on the nature of the transition. For example, a transition which involves a rearrangement of the classroom from seatwork to small groups takes more time to orchestrate than a transition between discussing one topic and another. Teachers have to consider a number of decisions which affect how transitions will be handled:

- How will the momentum of the lesson be maintained while grouping arrangements are changed?
- What will students be doing in between activities?
- When should students be told what the goals of an activity are?

Teachers report a number of solutions to these questions:

I always think ahead and plan how I will handle transition times. For example, I might write an assignment for an exercise on the board so that some students can start the assignment while others are still getting their books.

I write my objectives for the lesson on the board so students can see how the different activities in the lesson are connected.

At the beginning of each new term for each of my classes, I work out rules and routines for things like passing out books, moving into groups, and handing in assignments.

Discussion

1. Consider a typical lesson that you teach (or observe), such as a reading, writing, listening, or speaking lesson. What format does this kind of lesson typically follow (i.e., what typical sequence of activities makes up the lesson)? What principles or beliefs account for this format?
2. If you are teaching a class, have you developed a personalized format for lessons you teach regularly? What does the format consist of? Why does it have the format it does? Compare it with other formats used by teachers teaching the same kind of lesson. If you are observing a class, has the teacher developed a personalized format for it?
3. What are the advantages for learners of using established lesson formats? What advantages are there for teachers? Are there any disadvantages of using established formats?
4. Choose a method you are familiar with that has not been discussed in this chapter (e.g., Audiolingual Method and Silent Way). What does the format for a typical lesson consist of?
5. Do you (or a teacher whose class you are observing) use routines for handling transition times? What routines are effective?

Pacing

Since the formats used for most language lessons consist of a sequence of sub-activities which address the overall goals of the lesson, deciding how much time to allocate to each sub-activity is an important issue in teaching. *Pacing* is the extent to which a lesson maintains its momentum and communicates a sense of development. How much time to allocate to each part of the lesson is thus an important decision which teachers must make while planning or teaching a lesson. Decisions related to pacing are important aspects of interactive decision making, since teaching involves monitoring students' engagement in learning tasks and deciding when it is time to bring a task to completion and move on to another activity before students' attention begins to fade.

Various suggestions are given concerning pacing in articles on teacher training. Strategies recommended to help achieve suitable pacing within lessons often include:

- Avoiding needless or over-lengthy explanations and instructions, and letting students get on with the job of learning.
- Using a variety of activities within a lesson, rather than spending the whole lesson on one activity.
- Avoiding predictable and repetitive activities, where possible.
- Selecting activities of an appropriate level of difficulty.
- Setting a goal and time limit for activities: activities that have no obvious conclusion or in which no time frame is set tend to have little momentum.
- Monitoring students' performance on activities to ensure that students have had sufficient but not too much time.

In a study of an effective ESL reading teacher, Richards (1990) identified pacing as one of the significant features of the teacher's lessons. This was achieved through including a variety of activities within each lesson.

The teacher provides a variety of different learning experiences within lessons. In the lesson observed, four different activities were used, and this variation in activities may have contributed to the positive attitude of the students toward the classroom tasks as well as the active pacing of the lesson.   (p. 96)

Tikunoff (1985a) points out that pacing is sometimes teacher controlled and at other times student directed.

In some situations, pacing may need to be completely under control of the teacher; no student may move to the next task until given instructions to do so. In other situations, however, pacing might be negotiable, particularly if several tasks are underway concurrently. In this case, an understanding must exist of the optimal time one can spend on a task, and the time by when it is expected to be completed. Many teachers increase options in this area by negotiating contracts with students which include, among other things, the time by which a task will be accomplished.   (pp. 62–3)

Pacing is identified as a basic teaching skill in manuals for pre-service training of ESL/EFL teachers. For example, Gower and Walters (1983: 43–4), in discussing classroom management, comment:

You must get the timing right. If the activity lasts too long, it'll drag. If it doesn't last long enough, it won't give any sense of satisfaction. If one group finishes early, give it a further activity, related to the task. Alternatively, you may wish to stop all the groups at that point. But don't let a group or pair sit around with nothing to do. Generally it's better to stop an activity when it's going well, provided it has achieved its broad aims, than to let it peter out.

Discussion

1. Do you think a lesson that has a fairly rapid pacing is necessarily better than one that does not? Why or why not?
2. Suggest one or two ways that a teacher could monitor his or her pacing of lessons.
3. Suggest one or two ways that a teacher could improve pacing in his or her lessons.
4. Pacing is one way in which the momentum of a lesson is achieved. What other factors contribute to the momentum of lessons?

Closure

Another important dimension of structuring is bringing a lesson to a close effectively. Closure refers to those concluding parts of a lesson which serve to (a) reinforce what has been learned in a lesson, (b) integrate and review the content of a lesson, and (c) prepare the students for further learning. Several strategies are available to create an effective lesson closure. These strategies not only help facilitate learning of the content of the lesson, but also allow the lesson to be seen as an integrated whole. Strategies which teachers use to achieve closure include:

- Summarizing what has been covered in the lesson.
- Reviewing key points of the lesson.
- Relating the lesson to the course or lesson goals.
- Pointing out links between the lesson and previous lessons.
- Showing how the lesson relates to students' real-world needs.
- Making links to a forthcoming lesson.
- Praising students for what they have accomplished during the lesson.

The particular kind of strategy used will vary according to the type of lesson (e.g., a discussion activity or a lecture), as well as the level of the class. For example, with a discussion activity the closure typically involves summarizing the main points brought up by the students in their discussion, relating the discussion to lesson goals and previous learning, or applying the discussion outcomes to other situations. This type of closure serves to summarize and synthesize ideas, points of view, generalizations, and conclusions. It is often an important part of learning since it can "bring it all together" for students who may have been confused during the discussion.

A different approach to closure would be appropriate in a lecture, which is a much more teacher-centered, one-way presentation of information. Typically the closure sequence of a lecture serves to reinforce what has been presented with a review of key points covered in the lecture. This may include questioning by the teacher to determine how much the students have understood. Often the closure will include a transition to the next lesson in which the students will be assigned a problem to think about or a task that will help provide an entry to the next lecture.

Discussion

1. Review the list of strategies for lesson closures in this section. Can you think of other strategies of this kind? Which strategies do you think you use most often in the kind of classes you teach?
2. Suggest closure strategies that might be appropriate for these kinds of lessons: (a) a composition class focusing on writing cause and effect paragraphs, (b) a class debate on a topic related to the environment, (c) a reading class focusing on strategies for faster reading.
3. You have been asked to teach a two-hour lesson for an intermediate conversation class focusing on making requests and offers. What types of activities will you include in your lesson? How will these activities be sequenced? What kind of opening and closure will you use?

Follow-up activities

Journal activities

In your journal this week, describe how structuring was achieved in your lessons or in the lessons you observed. How did the lessons open? How were the activities sequenced? How was pacing achieved? How did the lessons close? How effective do you think the structuring of the lessons was?

Classroom observation tasks

1. Observe a language lesson. What strategy or strategies does the teacher use to begin and end the lesson? How is the lesson divided into sections? Then interview the teacher about the lesson. What rationale does the teacher give for the lesson organization?
2. Observe a lesson from the point of view of transitions. How does the teacher handle transitions from one sub-activity to another?
3. Observe a lesson from the point of view of pacing. Was the pacing of the lesson effective? If so, how did the teacher achieve it? Which of the strategies given on page 123 did the teacher use?

Lesson-report task

Use the lesson-report form in Appendix 5 to monitor your teaching over a one-week period from the point of view of openings, sequencing, pacing, and closure. Compare the information you collect with another teacher's self-report information. How similar are the strategies you use?

Action research case study #4

Transitions during lessons

This project was conducted by a secondary school teacher in an EFL context.

INITIAL REFLECTION

I teach a very large English class (44 students) in a secondary school. The students in my class are hard-working. They are very good at rote-learning, but are not used to communicative activities. Whenever I try to set up pair work or group work, it seems that it takes the students a very long time to reorganize and get started on the task. As a result, the bell would often ring before students could finish the activities that I wanted them to complete for that lesson. I feel this is because I am not managing the transitions between activities very effectively, and thus a lot of time is wasted.

PLANNING

I decided I needed to make a plan of action to help students move more quickly into their groups and get started on their tasks. I planned to do two things differently in my class. First, I decided to set up permanent groups, so that students would always know who they would be working with. Next, I planned to monitor my instructions to make sure the directions given to students were clear and students could understand what they were supposed to do.

I also set up a plan to monitor the results of these changes. I decided that after every lesson, I would take two minutes to write down my thoughts about how effective I thought the transitions during the lesson were and why the transition was either effective or not effective. I also decided to ask a colleague to come in and observe my class once a month to see how I handled transitions, using a form that I adapted from Good and Brophy (1987).

ACTION

The following lesson, I discussed this problem with my students and told them I thought sometimes it took too long to move from one activity to another. I asked them how they felt about it, and they agreed that too much time was wasted in class. I then told them about my idea for setting up permanent groups, and they agreed that it was a good idea. The students formed groups for the activity I had planned, and then when they finished the activity I told them these would now be permanent arrangements for any group work done in class.

OBSERVATION

I kept notes over the next two weeks about the transition times in class. From a review of these notes, it seems that the transitions were now more effective. Students moved into their groups immediately whenever I told them we would be doing group work. I also found that my directions were simple enough for the students to understand, perhaps because they were now used to the routine of doing group work and didn't need so much explanation.

Two weeks after implementing my action plan, I asked a colleague to come and observe my class. My colleague confirmed that students moved quickly into their groups and that my directions were very clear.

However, the observer pointed out three other areas that could improve the transitions in my class. First, he observed that sometimes I gave no advance warning for the students to finish up one activity, so that it took some groups longer to move on to the next activity. Second, he observed that the materials students needed to use were stored in hard-to-reach places. Third, he observed that a few groups would finish early and would just sit quietly doing nothing until the other groups had finished and I gave directions for the next activity.

REFLECTION

From this information, it seems that the original plan that I had put into operation was effective. I had achieved my objectives of moving students into their groups more quickly and giving clearer directions. Because of this, students are spending more time on the activities that I assign them, and are able to complete the activities within the period of the lesson.

However, there still seems room for improvement in my classroom management. I have developed a new plan based on the information collected by my colleague. First of all, I have decided to set specific time limits for any group work that I assign to students and give them a one-minute warning signal before the time is up. Second, I plan to put an empty desk in the front center of the room, and use this desk to place all the materials that will be needed for the lesson so that both students and myself will have easy access to them when we need them. Third, I will plan additional activities that students can do if they finish early so that they will not just be sitting and waiting for the others to finish.

Appendix 1: Lesson beginnings – relating activities to purpose

PURPOSES	ILLUSTRATIVE ACTIVITIES
I to establish appropriate AFFECTIVE FRAMEWORK	
a create friendly, relaxed atmosphere	music, introductions, greetings, joke, chat (personal, topical)
b create suitable physical environ.	get ss to arrange furniture
c focus attention	greetings, listening activity, visual stimulus (incl. video)
d make class enjoyable	game, lighthearted oral activity
e get everyone involved	game, pairwork activity, go over homework
f raise confidence	chat (familiar questions, topical issues), controlled activities, review, homework (because prepared), plenary choral activity
g stimulate interest	anything lively or unusual - vary the beginning!
II to establish appropriate COGNITIVE FRAMEWORK	
a provide organizing framework	make connections with last lesson, describe activities or objectives for part of/whole lesson, introduce topic
b stimulate awareness of need (ling/cult.)	questions (e.g. based on picture), quiz
c elicit relevant linguistic knowl.	brainstorming, oral activity
d elicit relevant experience	questions
III to encourage STUDENT RESPONSIBILITY and INDEPENDENCE	
a make ss aware of learning skills and strategies	consciousness-raising activities (e.g. memorization game), elicitation of ss' individual strategies
IV to fulfill REQUIRED INSTITUTIONAL ROLE	
a give feedback	go through (previous) homework
b check on previous learning	quiz, game, brainstorm, ask for summary, questions, check homework
c give value for time/money	(This has more to do with how you start - e.g. punctuality and relevance - than what you do)
V to overcome PRAGMATIC DIFFICULTY	
a mimimise problems of (and for) ss arriving late	short (e.g. revision) activities, chat

(Reprinted with permission from I. McGrath, S. Davies, and H. Mulphin, 1992, "Lesson beginnings," *Edinburgh Working Papers in Applied Linguistic,* Department of Applied Linguistics/Institute for Applied Language Studies, University of Edinburgh, Scotland.)

Appendix 2: Sequence of activities in a communicative lesson

---

8 *Giving opinions, agreeing and disagreeing, discussing*

8.1   *Conversation* 🔲

Sue: Well Ken, if you ask me, there's too much violence on television. Why, killing seems normal now.

Ken: Uh Sue, I'm not sure if I agree with you. I've never read any proof that supports your claim.

Sue: Oh Ken, it's common sense. The point is, is if you keep seeing shootings and muggings and stranglings, you won't care if it happens on your street.

Mary: I think that's interesting.

Ken: Maybe, but ... I've never met people that are that apathetic about violence.

Sue: Oh I'm sorry, I don't see what you mean. Would you mind explaining that point?

Ken: Let me put it another way, Sue. The people on my street – they're not influenced by what happens on television.

Sue: Oh, but people may care about violence on their street, but not about violence in general.

Ken: Wouldn't you say that ... television is just a passive way of letting off steam?

Sue: Oh Ken, that's exactly what I mean! People watching violence to cool off proves my point – they get used to violence!

Mary: I think that's a good point, Sue. I mean, Ken, don't you see what she's saying?

Sue: Yes! There's got to be a better way to cool off!

Mary: I agree. Well, like talking with friends, or sports, or reading, or ...

Ken: I agree with you, Mary. Anyway, TV's really boring, so why argue about it?

Sue: [*laughs*] I agree with you there.

Mary: [*laughs*] That's true.

(Reprinted with permission from L. Jones and C. von Bayer, 1983, *Functions of American English*, pp. 43–5, published by Cambridge University Press.)

8.2 *Presentation: giving opinions* 📻

When you are taking part in a discussion it is useful to have techniques up your sleeve for getting people to listen to you and to give yourself *thinking time* while you arrange your ideas. Here are some useful opening expressions (they get more and more formal as you go down the list):

INFORMAL *If you ask me ...*
  You know what I think? I think that ...
  The point is ...
  Wouldn't you say that ... ?
  Don't you agree that ... ?
  As I see it ...
  I'd just like to say that I think that ...
FORMAL *I'd like to point out that ...*

Decide with your teacher when these different expressions would be appropriate. Do you agree with the order they have been put in? Can you suggest more expressions?

8.3 *Exercise*

Make up conversations from the cues below, using expressions presented in 8.2. Follow this pattern:

📻 A: How do you feel about big dogs?
  B: Well, if you ask me, big dogs are a nuisance.
  A: Why do you think that?
  B: Because they eat a lot of food, and run around where they're not wanted, and ...

big dogs   foreign travel
cats   learning a foreign language
daycare   downtown parking spaces
women drivers   transistor radios
capital punishment   children

Try to use new expressions each time!

8.4 *Exercise*

Work in groups of three. Find out each other's opinions on these subjects:

vacations   inflation
birthdays   air travel
Christmas   television
politeness   winter sports
lotteries   communism

Report your partners' opinions to the students in another group.

Appendix 3: Sequence of activities in a process writing lesson

Part I Introduction to Writing Processes:
Writing from Observation and Experience 1

Unit 1 *Getting to Draft* 3

Chapter 1 Preliminaries 4
Chapter 2 Getting Ideas 7
Chapter 3 Preparing for a Draft .28
Chapter 4 Writing a First Draft 47

Unit 2 *Working with a Draft* 63

Chapter 5 Focusing on Main Ideas 64
Chapter 6 Developing and Shaping Ideas 82
Chapter 7 Beginning and Ending Drafts 105

Unit 3 *Reworking the Draft* 121

Chapter 8 Revising 122
Chapter 9 Polishing Revised Drafts 135

(Reprinted with permission from I. Leki, 1989, *Academic Writing-Techniques and Tasks,* p. xi, St. Martin's Press, New York.)

Appendix 4: Sequence of activities in a reading lesson

UNIT ONE

A Place of Your Own

Section 1   Leaving Home

What do you think?

1   Young school leavers in Britain sometimes leave home to live elsewhere. Why do you think this happens? Do you think it is common? Note down your ideas briefly.

The extract below comes from an article in a magazine for young people in Britain about to leave school.

2   What are the advantages and disadvantages of living at home once you are grown up? Consider especially the following: – comfort
         – expense
         – independence
         – friends

3   Next, make your own personal list of advantages and disadvantages.

4   Now read the first three paragraphs and note the advantages and disadvantages of living at home which are mentioned. Did you think of these?

A person's home is as much a reflection of his personality as the clothes he wears, the food he eats and the friends with whom he spends his time. Depending on personality, how
5   people see themselves and how they allow others to see them, most have in mind an 'ideal home'. But in general, and especially for the student or new wage earners, there are practical limitations of cash and location on achieving that idea.

Cash shortage, in fact, often means that the only way of
10   getting along when you leave school is to stay at home for a while until things improve financially. There are obvious advantages to living at home – personal laundry is usually still done along with the family wash, meals are provided and there will be a well-established circle of friends to call upon.
15   Parents are often quite generous in asking for a minimum rent, and there is rarely the responsibility for paying fuel bills, rates etc.

(*continued*)

UNIT ONE

On the other hand, much depends on how a family gets on.
Do your parents like your friends? You may love you family –
20   but do you like them? Are you prepared to be tolerant when
your parents ask where you are going in the evening and
what time you expect to be back? Do they mind if you want to
throw a party? If you find you can't manage a workable
compromise, and that you finally have the money to leave,
25   how do you go about finding somewhere else to live?

5   How *do* you find somewhere else?
Think of three possible ways of finding a place to live.

6   Now read on. . . .

If you plan to stay in your home area, the possibilities are
probably well-known to you already. Friends and the local
paper are always a good source of information. If you are
going to work in a new area, again there are the papers – and
30   the accommodation agencies, though these should be
approached with caution. Agencies are allowed to charge a
fee, usually the equivalent of the first week's rent, if you take
accommodation they have found for you. But some less
scrupulous operators may charge you a fee to look at
30   accommodation which may be already occupied when you get
there!

For students, many colleges, polytechnics and universities
have accommodation officers who will do the necessary
hunting. This is a difficult job in some areas where there is a
40   large student population with scant residential provision and
few locals who are keen to take students as tenants or
boarders. But what sort of accommodation is available?

7   Before reading further, list the different kinds of
accommodation you think might be available for young people in Britain.

8   Now read on, ticking off the items on your list as they are
mentioned and adding any you had not thought of.

If you like the idea of living with a family (other than your
own), or in a small house where there are a few other
45   boarders, digs might be the answer. Good landladies – those
who are superb cooks, launderers and surrogate mothers, are
figures as popular in fiction as the bad ones who terrorise
their guests and overcharge them at the slightest opportunity.
The truth is probably somewhere between the two extremes
50   If you are lucky, the food will be adequate, some of your
laundry may be done for you and you will have a reasonable
amount of comfort and companionship. For the less fortunate
digs may be lonely, house rules may restrict the freedom to
invite friends to visit, and shared cooking and bathroom
55   facilities can be frustrating and row-provoking if tidy and
untidy guests are living under the same roof.

2

The same disadvantages can apply to flatsharing, with the added difficulties which arise from deciding who pays for what, and in what proportion. One person may spend hours
60 on the phone or wallowing in deep, hot baths, while another rarely makes calls and takes cold showers. If you want privacy with a guest, how do you persuade the others to go out; how do you persuade them to leave you in peace, especially if you are a student and want to study.

65 Conversely, flat sharing can be very cheap, there will always be someone to talk to and go out with, and the chores, in theory, can be shared. Even so, if you value privacy and a place of your own where you can put up your own posters, play your favourite music, etc, perhaps it would be better to
70 look for a bedsitter or a flat of your own.

The beauty of a bedsit is its simplicity. It is relatively cheap, easy to keep clean, economical to heat since it is usually a single room, and at its best a 'cosy' place to live. At its worst, the bedsit can be cramped and impregnated with cooking
75 smells or cluttered with damp washing. It can also be very lonely if you are not naturally sociable and have moved to a new area.

A flat will usually give you more space, but you will have to pay for it, and, like the bedsitter, it can be a lonely start in a
80 extra expense of a flat can be minimal. You will probably have your own washing and cooking facilities, and if the flat is not furnished, there is the fun of going to auctions and junk shops to choose your own furniture.

from *Prospect*, 1977

Check your understanding

KEY 9 Answer these questions. First locate the right part of the text, and then read that part carefully.
a) What are the disadvantages of a bedsitter?
b) Name two problems flatsharers might have.
c) What do living in good digs and living at home have in common?
d) For what kind of person might a bedsitter be a bad thing?
e) What kind of person might prefer a bedsitter to a shared flat?

KEY 10 Which of the following six statements do you think best sums up the author's point of view?
i) There are few advantages in living at home after leaving school.
ii) Accommodation agencies are the best source of help when looking for somewhere to live.

(continued)

UNIT ONE

iii) If one cannot live at home the best arrangement is to
find a good landlady.
iv) One should carefully consider the advantages and
disadvantages of all kinds of home before making a
decision.
v) Living away from home is very lonely.
vi) Finding a flat of your own is the best solution of all.

What do you think?

Is the situation described in the extract similar to that in
your country? *Do* young people move away from home,
and if so, where do they move to?

(From P. Barr, J. Clegg, and C. Wallace, 1981, *Advanced Reading Skills*, pp. 1–4,
Longman, Essex.)

Appendix 5: Lesson-report form for structuring of lessons

CLASS _____ DATE _____
GOALS AND CONTENT OF LESSON _____

OPENINGS

The activity I used to open the lesson was _____
The purpose of this activity was _____
The effectiveness of this opening was:
   a) very effective
   b) moderately effective
   c) not very effective

SEQUENCING

The lesson contained the following sequence of activities: _____

_____
The purpose of sequencing the lesson in this way was: _____

_____
The effectiveness of this sequence was:
   a) very effective
   b) moderately effective
   c) not very effective

PACING:

Strategies I use to achieve pacing were _____
The effectiveness of this strategy was:
   a) very effective
   b) moderately effective
   c) not very effective

CLOSURE:

The activity I used to end the lesson was _____
The purpose of this activity was _____
The effectiveness of this closure was:
   a) very effective
   b) moderately effective
   c) not very effective

7 Interaction in the second language classroom

A common theme underlying different methods of language teaching is that second language learning is a highly interactive process. A great deal of time in teaching is devoted both to interaction between the teacher and the learners, and to interaction among the learners themselves. The quality of this interaction is thought to have a considerable influence on learning (Ellis 1985). The focus in this chapter is on the nature of classroom interaction and how teachers can influence the kind of interaction that occurs in their own classrooms. These issues will be explored through examining the teacher's action zone within the class, learners' interactional competence, learner's interactional styles, and the effects of grouping arrangements on classroom interaction.

The teacher's action zone

The following notes were written by a teacher after teaching a lesson.

Today I taught a lesson around a discussion on an environmental issue. The lesson went very well. First, I introduced the topic by talking about environmental problems in our city and got students to give examples of the major environmental problems we face. This got lots of comments from the class and everybody had an opportunity to say something and express an opinion. After ten minutes I divided the students into small groups and asked them to come up with a solution to one of the problems we talked about. During this time I moved around the class, monitoring the students' language use and giving feedback. After twenty minutes I got the group leaders to report their groups' recommendations and I wrote key points on the board.

The following comments on the same lesson were written by an observer:

When you were speaking to the whole class, the students in the middle
  front row seats answered most of your questions.
When you moved around the class you spent much more time with
  some groups than with others.

These different perceptions of a lesson highlight the fact that despite a
teacher's best intentions, teachers sometimes interact with some students
in the class more frequently than others. Although teachers generally try
to treat students fairly and give every student in the class an equal
opportunity to participate in the lesson, it is often hard to avoid interacting with some students more than others. This creates what is referred to
as the teacher's *action zone*. An action zone is indicated by:

those students with whom the teacher regularly enters into eye
  contact;
those students to whom the teacher addresses questions; and
those students who are nominated to take an active part in the lesson.

These students are located within the teacher's action zone and are likely
to participate more actively in a lesson than students who fall outside the
action zone. In many classrooms, this zone includes the middle front row
seats and the seats up the middle aisle. If a teacher is teaching from the
front of the class, students seated there are more likely to have the
opportunity to participate actively in the lesson because of their prox-
imity to the teacher (Adams and Biddle 1970). However, teachers often
have their own personal action zones. For example, a teacher may:

look more often to the right hand side of the class than to the left,
call on girls more often than boys,
call on students of one ethnic background more often than those of
  another,
call on students whose names are easy to remember,
call on brighter students more often than others, or
in a mainstream class containing students with limited English proficiency, tend to focus attention on the first language speakers in the
  classroom and to make relatively few demands on the others
  (Schinke-Llano 1983).

Figure 1 shows a teacher's action zone as recorded by an observer who
marked on a seating plan the number of times the teacher addressed the
whole class and individual students in the class, as well as the number of
times individual students interacted with the teacher.

Although a teacher may feel that all the students in the class have an
equal opportunity to participate in the lesson, Figure 1 shows that this is

This observation form uses a seating plan of the classroom. The observer marks interaction patterns with an arrow each time an interaction occurs. The lines across the arrows indicate the number of interactions that occurred in the lesson.

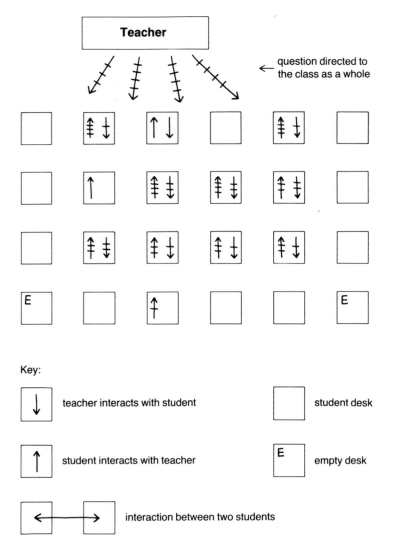

Figure 1   The teacher's interaction with students during a lesson.

not always so. During this lesson, the teacher addressed the whole class nineteen times and interacted with only twelve of the twenty-two individuals. It also seems that the teacher overlooked the students sitting in the right and left rows, and had an action zone located in the center of the room. If active participation is important in learning, then those students not within the teacher's action zone are at a disadvantage.

Discussion

1. If you are teaching a class, do you think you have a clearly defined action zone when you teach? Does it favor some students in the class more than others? If so, how could you change your action zone? If you are observing a class, does the teacher have a defined action zone?
2. Some learners are often eager to be within the teacher's action zone because they like to play an active and public role in the lesson. Others are happy to be outside the teacher's action zone. Should all students be active and public participants in lessons? Why or why not?

Interactional competence

While teachers need to be able to manage their interaction with the class in a way which allows all students equal opportunities to participate, learners also need to learn how they are expected to interact in the classroom. This has been described as a learner's *interactional competence* (Tikunoff 1985a,b), which involves learning particular patterns of interaction and behavior both vis-à-vis the other students in the class as well as with the teacher. Interactional competence includes several dimensions of classroom behavior.

Knowing the etiquette of classroom interaction

Teachers establish their own rules for appropriate classroom behavior. For example, in some classrooms, when the teacher enters the room at the beginning of a lesson, students stand at attention, greet the teacher in unison, and sit down to wait for instructions. When they wish to ask a question, they raise their hand. When asked a question, they stand to give the answer. At the end of the lesson, they wait for the teacher to dismiss them before leaving the room. In other, less traditional classrooms, however, students are often engaged in classroom tasks before the teacher enters the room. If so, the teacher waits for a suitable moment to introduce a new teaching point. Students do not raise their hands when asking a question, but get the teacher's attention by calling out, "Excuse me." When students wish to leave their desk to consult another student, they do so without asking the teacher's permission. At the end of the lesson, students leave when they have completed their assignments, without waiting for a formal dismissal from the teacher.

Knowing the rules for individual and collaborative work

Students also need to know when they should work individually on a task and when it is appropriate to seek other students' assistance or cooperation. Individual teachers establish their own rules and procedures for class work. However, when students are unclear as to what the teacher's rules are, they may behave in ways that the teacher finds inappropriate. This is seen in the following comments by a teacher:

Some of my students can be a problem because they like to get up and wander around the room when I ask them to do an assignment. They seem to be more interested in talking to other students about their assignments than in getting help from me.

These learner behaviors may be influenced by cultural factors (see Chapter 5). For example, Phillips (1972: 377) noted the following differences between the classroom behavior of American Indian children and non-Indian children:

There is, on the part of Indian students, relatively less interest, desire, and/or ability to internalize and act in accordance with some of the basic rules underlying classroom maintenance of orderly interaction. Most notably, Indian students are less willing than non-Indian students to accept the teacher as director and controller of all classroom activities. They are less interested in developing the one-to-one communicative relationship between teacher and student, and more interested in maintaining and developing relationships with their peers, regardless of what is going on in the classroom.

While some teachers establish expectations and procedures for appropriate classroom behavior very early on with a new group of students, others do not make their expectations clear, which can lead to confusion on both the teacher's and the learners' parts.

Knowing when to ask and answer questions

Teachers generally expect learners to ask questions during a lesson, although the extent to which they encourage active student participation may differ from one teacher to another and from one culture to another. On entering a new class, a priority for learners is to establish what their expected level of participation is and when and how they should interrupt the teacher to ask questions. Teachers may have their own preferences for when students should or should not ask questions. For example, some teachers prefer setting aside a particular question segment within a lesson, rather than allowing the flow of the lesson to be interrupted by questions. Other teachers prefer students to ask questions as they arise. Students may also have different expectations about how to answer questions from their teachers. In some cultures, students are expected to wait until called on and to answer only when they are sure of being right. In language classrooms, however, students are generally expected to participate actively, since answering questions is often regarded as a way of practicing the language.

Knowing how and when to get assistance or feedback in completing a task

Learners also have to learn what rules operate for getting help during a lesson. Should they ask the teacher? Should they turn to another student? Or should they keep silent to avoid disrupting others? Tikunoff (1985b) studied students in bilingual classrooms in the United States to see how students knew if they were doing well on completing a class task and where they went for help in the case of difficulty. Successful students seemed to be aware of when they needed help as well as how to get it. This is seen in the following comments from learners:

When I don't know how to do something, the teacher helps me, but it's
  OK not to go to the teacher if you don't need help.
The teacher helps me when I need it, but it's OK for friends to help
  too.
The teacher helps me during recess as well as after school if I need it.

Knowing appropriate rules for displaying knowledge

Although classrooms are places where students are expected to learn, there are rules which govern how one should display the result of what one has learned. Some teachers, particularly teachers from a Western culture, encourage learners to display what they have learned in front of their peers. When a teacher asks a question and a student in the class knows the answer, the teacher normally expects the student to answer the question. However, students from some cultures may feel that publicly displaying one's knowledge in this way would be seen by their peers as showing off; hence, they might avoid answering the question. Public display of knowledge, however, was found to be highly valued by some students in the reading class studied by Bondy (1990). She found that public demonstration of the ability to read was a source of status for some students in the class. They made comments in front of other children which drew attention to the fact that they could read and successfully engage in reading activities. "Reading seemed to be an activity done for praise, reward, and public recognition" (p. 36).

The process of arriving at a shared understanding of the appropriate rules for displaying knowledge in a classroom is clearly an important issue for teachers and learners. It may take some time for teachers and students to discover what assumptions govern the other party's behavior.

Discussion

1. What rules govern the etiquette of classroom interaction in your country or institution?
2. If you are teaching a class, do you have a code of etiquette for your classroom? In what way does it reflect your view of your role as a teacher? If you are observing a class, what is the teacher's code of etiquette?
3. Can you give further examples which show how cultural factors in a context you are familiar with influence the interactional competence of language learners?

Learner interactional patterns

The concept of interactional competence refers to the rules that students are expected to follow in order to participate appropriately in lessons. However, because of individual differences in learners' personalities and their individual cognitive styles, different patterns of interaction can often be observed among learners in any one class. Good and Power (1976) describe six different interactional patterns. The first four of these can be seen to reflect how the four cognitive styles discussed in Chapter 3 can lead to particular patterns of classroom behavior. The last two interactional styles describe negative reactions to schooling and hence cannot be linked to the four cognitive styles discussed earlier.

Task-oriented students (c.f. Concrete Learning Style). These students are generally highly competent and successful in completing academic tasks. They enter into learning tasks actively and generally complete tasks with a high degree of accuracy. They enjoy school and learning. They seldom need a teacher's help, but if they feel they need it they do not hesitate to ask for it. They are cooperative students and create few discipline problems.

Phantom students (c.f. Analytical Learning Style). These students may not often be noticed or heard in the classroom, although they are generally good students who work steadily on classroom tasks. However, they participate actively in lessons only infrequently, and rarely initiate conversation or ask for help. Because they do not disrupt the class or other students, teachers and other students do not know them very well.

Social students (c.f. Communicative Learning Style). These students place a high value on personal interaction. Although they are competent in accomplishing classroom tasks, they tend to value socializing with friends more than completing class assignments. They enjoy tutoring others in the class and participate actively in the lesson, although their answers may not always be correct. They tend to be popular with their classmates, but they may be less popular with their teachers because their approach to learning can create classroom management problems. They sometimes talk too much and do not hesitate to seek assistance from the teacher or other classmates when they need it.

Dependent students (c.f. Authority-oriented Learning Style). These students need the teacher's support and guidance to complete class tasks and tend not to maintain engagement on tasks without frequent reinforcement and support. They need structure and guidance in completing tasks and tend not to work well in large groups. They often depend on the teacher or other students to tell them if their learning has been successful and if not, how to remedy the problem.

Isolated students. These students set themselves apart from others and withdraw from classroom interactions. They may avoid learning situations by turning away from activities such as peer or group work. They show reluctance to sharing their work with others or allowing others to respond to it. Consequently they tend to be less proficient in completing learning tasks.

Alienated students. These students react against teaching and learning and are often hostile and aggressive. They create discipline problems and make it difficult for those around them to work. They require close supervision, and their learning problems are often related to personal problems.

While classifications such as these capture some useful generalizations about student interaction patterns in the classroom, most systems of this kind are somewhat arbitrary, and students may not be classified easily in one category or another. They may favor one interactional style for one particular learning task and then adopt a different style for a different task, for example. The usefulness of classification systems such as this is simply to serve as a reminder that individual students may favor different interactional styles and that there is no single interactional style that can be regarded as ideal for all students.

Discussion

1. Do you think the differences between Task-oriented, Phantom, Social, and Dependent students apply to students in a class you are familiar with? If not, what other kinds of differences in interactional style occur among the students?
2. Reflect on your own approach to learning. How would you describe your own interactional style?
3. What type of interactional style do you encourage among students in your class (or would you encourage in learners)? Do you think you tend to behave differently to students according to differences in their preferred interactional style?
4. With a partner, develop a questionnaire that could be used to identify the preferred interactional style of learners.

Grouping arrangements

While learners may have individual preferences for the kind of interactional style they favor in the classroom, the interactional dynamics of a classroom are largely a product of choices the teacher makes about the learning arrangements he or she sets up within a lesson. Most teachers use the following learning arrangements depending on the kind of lesson they are teaching, though teachers use some more frequently than others.

Whole-class teaching. The teacher leads the whole class through a learning task. For example, the teacher conducts a class discussion

of an article from a newspaper, asking questions about it and eliciting comments around the class.

Individual work. Each student in the class works individually on a task
without interacting with peers or without public interaction with the
teacher. For example, students complete a grammar exercise by
going through a worksheet.

Pair work. Students work in pairs to complete a task.

Group work. Students work in groups on learning tasks.

Choosing grouping arrangements that are appropriate for specific learning tasks is an important decision. Some of the factors which affect
grouping arrangements will now be considered.

Whole-class teaching

Research on teaching suggests that whole-class instructional methods are
the most commonly used models in public school teaching, particularly
for the beginning of a lesson. In whole-class activities

the teacher typically begins a lesson by reviewing prerequisite material, then
introduces and develops new concepts or skills, then leads the group in a
recitation or supervised practice or application activity, and then assigns
seatwork or homework for students to do on their own. The teacher may
occasionally teach small groups rather than the whole class (especially for
beginning reading instruction) and may provide a degree of individualized
instruction when "making the rounds" during individual seatwork
times.   (Good and Brophy 1987: 353)

Researchers of classroom interaction have developed observational systems to describe and classify patterns of student-teacher interaction in
teacher-led whole-class activities. A well-known observation scheme
developed for observing teacher-student interaction in mainstream
classes uses seven categories for describing verbal exchanges (Brown
1975: 67):

TL   *Teacher lectures* – describes, explains, narrates, directs
TQ   *Teacher questions* about content or procedure, which pupils are
         intended to answer.
TR   *Teacher responds* – accepts feelings of the class; describes past
         feelings and future feelings in a non-threatening way.
         Praises, encourages, jokes with pupils.
         Accepts or uses pupils' ideas. Builds upon pupil responses. Uses
         mild criticism such as "no, not quite."

PR   *Pupils respond* directly and predictably to teacher questions and directions.

PV   *Pupils volunteer* information, comments, or questions.

S   *Silence* – pauses, short periods of silence.

X   *Unclassifiable*. Confusion in which communications cannot be understood. Unusual activities such as reprimanding or criticizing pupils. Demonstrating without accompanying teacher or pupil talk. Short spates of blackboard work without accompanying teacher or pupil talk.

When this system is applied to the description of what happens in whole-class teacher-led activities, the findings from both second language classrooms and first language classrooms are the same: about 70% of the classroom time is taken up by the teacher talking or asking questions (Chaudron 1988). This pattern is seen in Figure 2 (on pages 150 and 151), which gives examples of lesson segments coded at three-second intervals according to the system developed by Brown.

There are both advantages and disadvantages to whole-class teaching in language classes. Among the advantages are:

- It enables the teacher to teach large numbers of students at the same time. In some countries, classes of up to fifty or sixty students are common, necessitating the use of many whole-class activities.
- In situations where a mainstream classroom contains a number of ESL students, the ESL students can feel that they are a part of the mainstream group and are functioning under equal terms with them rather than being singled out for special treatment.
- It can serve as a preparation for subsequent activities which can be completed individually or in groups.

However, critics of whole-class teaching have pointed out a number of disadvantages.

- Such instruction is teacher-dominated, with little opportunity for active student participation.
- Teachers tend to interact with only a small number of students in the class, as is seen from studies of teachers' action zones.
- Whole-class teaching assumes that all students can proceed at the same pace. However, slower students may be lost, and brighter students may be held back.

Although teachers can adapt whole-class activities to encourage more student participation (for example, by stopping from time to time during an activity and asking students to compare a response with a partner), teachers need to include other types of teaching in their lessons to provide learners with a variety of opportunities for communicative interaction and individual language use within the classroom.

Individual work

Individual work, or "seatwork," is generally the second most frequently used teaching pattern in classrooms. It includes such activities as completing worksheets, reading a comprehension passage and answering questions, doing exercises from a text or workbook, and composition and essay writing. Among the advantages of individual work are:

- It provides learners with the opportunity to progress at their own speed and in their own way.
- It provides learners with opportunities to practice and apply skills they have learned.
- It enables teachers to assess student progress.
- It enables teachers to assign different activities to different learners based on individual abilities and needs.
- It can be used to prepare learners for an up-coming activity.

Among the disadvantages are:

- It provides little opportunity for interaction, both with the teacher and with other students.
- It is sometimes difficult to monitor what students are actually doing during individual work.
- Students may complete a task at different times and run out of things to do, creating a classroom management problem.

For individual work to be accomplished successfully, a number of characteristics of successful individual work have been identified (Good and Brophy 1987: 233–4):

- It should be planned so that it relates to other kinds of learning arrangements, rather than being an isolated "filler" activity.
- Students should be given specific tasks with clear goals. There should be monitoring and follow-up to determine if students understand the task or are completing it accurately.
- Tasks should be at the right level of difficulty.
- Students should know what to do when completing an activity.

Example 1

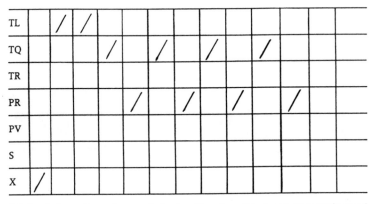

This is a drill type lesson. It occurs in simple arithmetic, and foreign language teaching and revision.

Example 2

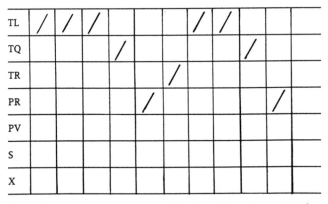

This is the most common pattern occurring in any lesson in any curriculum area. Brief teacher lectures followed by a question, a brief pupil response, a teacher response and more teacher talk.

Figure 2   Four lesson segments coded at three-second intervals. (Reprinted with permission from G. Brown, 1975, *Microteaching*, pp. 77–8, published by Methuen & Co.)

Example 3

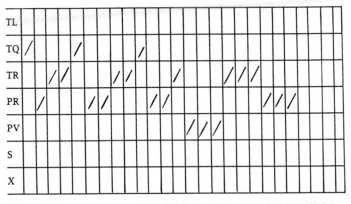

This is a fairly common pattern in English lessons. The sustained TRs usually bring forth PVs as well as PRs which the teacher then builds on.

Example 4

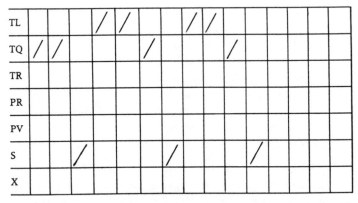

A beginner's lesson. Notice how he questions, receives no answer and rushes in with TLs. His pupils may be manipulating his behaviour. They keep quiet and he answers his own questions. This pattern then reinforces their silence keeping.

Figure 2 (*continued*)

Pair work

Despite the need for whole-class teaching and individual work in language classrooms, it has often been emphasized that without other kinds of interaction, students are deprived of many useful and motivating opportunities for using and learning the new language. Various alternatives have been proposed which emphasize the use of pairs and small groups in the classroom (e.g., Cooperative Learning, Collaborative Learning, and Communicative Language Teaching). Through interacting with other students in pairs or groups, students can be given the opportunity to draw on their linguistic resources in a nonthreatening situation and use them to complete different kinds of tasks. Indeed, it is through this kind of interaction that researchers believe many aspects of both linguistic and communicative competence are developed. "One learns how to do conversation, one learns how to interact verbally, out of this interaction syntactic structures are developed" (Hatch 1978: 404).

Both Long (1983) and Krashen (1985) have argued that when second language learners interact focusing on meaningful tasks or exchanges of information, then each learner receives (a) comprehensible input from his or her conversational partner, (b) a chance to ask for clarification as well as feedback on his or her output, (c) adjustment of the input to match the level of the learner's comprehension, and (d) the opportunity to develop new structures and conversational patterns through this process of interaction (see Figure 3). Long argues that use of carefully designed pair work tasks can help learners obtain "comprehensible input," that is, language that is at an appropriate level to facilitate acquisition. This input is obtained through the interactive negotiation learners take part in as they complete the task.

The following factors influence the nature of pair work tasks:

Information flow. For pair work tasks to promote better interaction, both students need to have different information that they are required to share in order to solve a problem or complete a task. Tasks with this type of information flow have been described as two-way tasks, while tasks in which one student has new information and presents it to his or her partner have been described as one-way tasks.

Product focus. Tasks are often more motivating if the result of the negotiation or interaction is some kind of product, such as a list, a map, a completed diagram, or a chart.

Choice of partner. Many different kinds of pairings are possible: for example, by mixed ability levels, shared ability levels, or mixed

Model of the relationship between type of conversational task and language acquisition

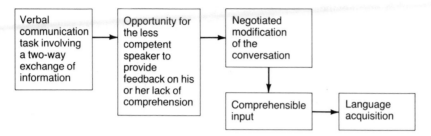

Figure 3   Model of the relationship between type of conversational task and language acquisition. (From Long, 1983: 214)

ethnic or language background. The need to change pairings from time to time is also an issue when pair work activities are used routinely.

Roles of partners. For some tasks both students may share a common role; for other tasks, one partner may serve as a peer tutor.

Group work

The use of group work activities is another frequently cited strategy for changing the interactional dynamics of language classrooms. In addition to the benefits of pair work activities, group work has a number of additional advantages.

- It reduces the dominance of the teacher over the class.
- It increases the amount of student participation in the class.
- It increases the opportunities for individual students to practice and use new features of the target language.
- It promotes collaboration among learners.
- It enables the teacher to work more as a facilitator and consultant.
- It can give learners a more active role in learning.

Successful group work activities involve decisions about the following factors:

Group size. An optimum size for group work needs to be determined based on the kind of task students are carrying out. If the group is too large, student interaction is affected; only a few students may participate, the others remaining silent or passive.

Purpose. Group activities need a goal, procedures, and a time frame to accomplish them, if they are to be focused and productive.

Roles. Decisions need to be made concerning the different roles of group members. Will they all have the same role? Are a group leader and secretary required? Will students take on different personas in completing a task?

The interactional dynamics of a lesson can thus be viewed as resulting from the interplay between the teacher's and the learners' interactional styles, the moment-to-moment demands of instruction, and the grouping arrangements that have been set up to facilitate teaching and learning. Lessons thus have a constantly changing interactional structure, which can either hinder or support effective language learning.

Discussion

1. What procedures can be used to minimize some of the potential disadvantages of whole-class teaching?
2. Learners sometimes resist pair or group activities because they prefer to learn from the teacher rather than from another language learner. Do you think this is a legitimate objection? How can it be addressed?
3. What are some of the implications of moving away from whole-class teaching to small group or pair activities? In what ways are the teacher's and learners' roles (a) threatened, and (b) empowered?

Follow-up activities

Journal activities

1. In your journal entries, focus on describing examples of how individual learners in your class (or in classes you observe) participate in lessons. You may wish to focus on two different kinds of students in a class, and describe their classroom interactional style over a period of time. Describe this and how it influences your (or the teacher's) interaction with the learners.
2. Over the next few lessons you teach (or observe), describe the extent to which you think you (or the teacher) managed to achieve a satisfactory level of interaction during the lessons. What strategies proved most effective in facilitating interaction within the class?

Investigation tasks

1. Observe learners completing a pair or group task. What kinds of negotiation did the task involve? Do you think this negotiation would facilitate language acquisition?
2. Read the following transcript of a lesson segment. Code the segment using Brown's observation scheme for observing teacher-student interaction discussed on pages 147–148. What does your coding indicate about the interactional patterns in this lesson?

LESSON TRANSCRIPT

[In this lesson, students are looking at material which has phonetic spellings of two characters, Benny and Penny, and drawings of the names of two objects, shirt and shorts.]

T: OK . . . who can make the first sentence here? . . . Who wants to make a sentence about Penny . . . or about . . . Abdullah, make a sentence about Penny please.
S1: What does Benn-
T: No, no questions yet. . . . just make a sentence.
S2: Which one?
T: No. . . . no questions.
S2: Ah. . . . it's Benny?
T: Yes, tell me something about Penny.
S2: Benny washing -
S3: IS washing. Benny IS washing.
S2: Uh, shirt . . . er . . . on the last day . . . the last day . . . on the last day . . . no.
T: Yesterday?
S2: Yes.
T: OK . . . What did he wash yesterday?
S2: He was wash- . . . er He washing.
T: Mohammed, can you help him?
S3: Penny washED his short . . . shirt.
T: Mm-hmm . . . we don't say washED though do we?
S3: washED.
T: No, just one syllable, we say washt.
S4: Wash.
S3: Washt.
S2: Washt.

T: And we say "tuh" . . . we write "ed," but we don't say washED . . . we say washT . . .
Ss: washT . . . washT . . . washT . . . washT.
T: Yes good, now Khalid, what did Penny do yesterday?
S2: He washt his shirt.
T: Good . . . Mohammed, can you make a sentence about Benny?
S3: He washed his shirt.
T: No, look at the picture.
S3: Oh, shorts, shorts, he washed his shorts.
T: That's right. Good.

Peer observation task

Ask a colleague to observe your class and to focus on your interaction with students in the class during a whole-class activity. The observer should note the frequency with which you interact with each student in the class. Then change roles and complete the same task for your partner. Did you teach to a restricted action zone? If not, how did you succeed in interacting with the whole class?

Observation tasks

1. Prepare a seating plan for a class you are observing like the one in Figure 1 on page 140. Code the teacher-to-class, teacher-to-student, and student-to-student interaction during a lesson. To what extent did the teacher succeed in involving all of the students in the class during the lesson?
2. Use the observation form in Appendix 1 to code part of a language lesson. (See pages 147–148 for an explanation of the coding system.) Does a pattern or style of interaction occur in the lesson? How would you describe it?

Lesson-report task

Use the lesson-report form in Appendix 2 to monitor the grouping arrangements used over a two-week period. How much variety is there in the grouping arrangements you use? How did the grouping arrangements contribute to the degree and quality of interaction among learners?

Action research case study #5

Grouping arrangements in the classroom

This project was carried out by a teacher in a private language school teaching adults in an EFL context.

INITIAL REFLECTION

I teach a class of mixed abilities and was worried about the amount of oral practice that less able students were getting during lessons. These students are generally reserved and reluctant to use English. Many of them also become embarrassed if they make a mistake when speaking in front of the other students. I wanted to find some way to boost the students' self-confidence, and thereby improve their fluency. I believe that using pair work is a good way of providing students with opportunities to practice English and regularly employ pair work in my class, but I was unsure about who the less able students should be paired with. I thought that if a less able student has a partner of better ability, the more fluent student might be able to help the other one during pair work. On the other hand, the less able student might feel embarrassed talking to such a student and might feel more comfortable working with a partner of the same ability. I decided to explore the effects of various types of pairing arrangements.

PLANNING AND ACTION

I began by giving students a questionnaire about their learning preferences and observing how much the less able students actually said in English during pair work. For two weeks, I noted when each student said a word, a phrase, a sentence, or several sentences in English and compared their performance in three different situations:

a less able student working with a more fluent student
a less able student working with a student of the same ability
a less able student working with the teacher

I also audio recorded one of the less able students when he was doing pair work in each of the above situations.

OBSERVATION

I was not surprised to find that students spoke the least amount of English when working with the teacher. However, I was very surprised to find out that the less able students spoke three times more English when working with a student of the same ability than when they had a more fluent partner. I concluded that the students were motivated to speak English, but perhaps felt intimidated when working with someone of much better ability.

While listening to the taped conversation of two less able students I observed that they generally took turns to speak, that no individual was dominant, and that they helped each other with vocabulary. The conversations were quite fluent and accurate. However, the tape of the less able student paired with the more fluent student indicated that, although the better student was very cooperative and tried to help his partner, he tended to dominate the conversation and overcorrect his partner without giving his partner much chance to practice.

From my questionnaire, I found out that students have more confidence to use English when they can help each other, when they have to be self-reliant, when the teacher is not always present, when they are not being corrected all the time, and when they are not being tested or monitored.

REFLECTION

During this investigation I learned a lot about my students' attitudes towards and abilities in using English. Gathering information from the students about how they use English was important to me. I discovered a way to deal with a class of mixed abilities and found a way to motivate and encourage my less able students. This project confirms my beliefs about the value of using pair work and has reduced my anxiety about pairing less able students together.

Appendix 1: Observation form

TL = Teacher describes, explains, narrates,
  directs
TQ = Teacher questions
TR = Teacher responds to pupil's response
PR = Pupil's response to teacher's questions
PV = Pupil volunteers information, comments
  or questions
S = Silence
X = Unclassifiable

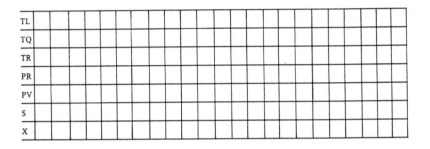

(Reprinted with permission from G. Brown, 1975, *Microteaching,* p. 70, published by Methuen & Co.)

Appendix 2: Lesson-report form for grouping arrangements

CLASS _____   DATE _____
GOALS AND CONTENT OF LESSON _____

Grouping Arrangements	Time Spent	Degree and Quality of Interaction
EXAMPLE: *Whole-class*	*10 minutes*	*students in front rows actively volunteering answers, but students in back of room not involved*

8 The nature of language learning activities

This chapter examines lessons in terms of the activities teachers use to achieve their instructional goals. An activity is described as a task that has been selected to achieve a particular teaching/learning goal. Research on teaching (e.g., Clark and Yinger 1979) suggests that the notion of activity is central to an understanding of teaching. It influences both how teachers conceptualize teaching as well as the ways they organize their lessons. In this chapter, the kinds of activities commonly used in ESL classes are described and the decisions that teachers have to consider when planning and using activities are discussed.

Lesson planning usually begins with consideration of general goals for a lesson, and then leads to decisions about the kinds of activities which will help attain these goals. Rather than breaking down the goals into behavioral objectives and then developing activities to match objectives, however, teachers often develop objectives as they plan specific teaching activities (see Chapter 4). According to Macdonald (1965) and Eisner (1967), it is while developing activities themselves that consideration of objectives becomes important, for this is where "ends for learning become integrated with means for learning" (Clark and Yinger 1979: 232). Activities are, hence, "the basic structural units of planning and action in the classroom" (Clark and Yinger 1979: 237). Nunan (1989b: 17) similarly observes:

[Teachers] tend to see lessons or units of work as the basic building blocks of their programmes. These lessons and units in turn are composed of sets of more or less integrated tasks and manipulative exercises of various sorts. The teacher's immediate preoccupation is thus with learning tasks and with integrating these into lessons and/or units.

The nature of language learning activities will now be examined in detail.

Types of language learning activities

Language teachers use many different kinds of approaches to teaching, depending on their assumptions and beliefs about how students learn and on the kind of methodology that they believe best supports this learning process. For example, in lessons based on a Situational Language Teaching approach, the sequence of classroom activities moves from presentation to controlled practice to free practice (see Chapter 6). In a Process Writing approach, activities move from pre-writing to drafting to revising. In skills classes, teachers often choose activities that support specific subskills or micro-skills, as is seen in the following two lesson plans:

Lesson Plan #1

Class:	Intermediate Reading/Writing	Week 6
Aims:	to practice reading strategies to practice summary writing	
Resources:	newspaper article on global changes in the weather; worksheet of comprehension questions	
Activities:		

1) Write headline of article on board. Students work in groups to predict four things the article might mention.
2) Distribute copies of the article. Students read within a five-minute period to identify the five main points of the article.
3) Students compare answers.
4) Students read the article again and answer comprehension questions on the worksheet.
5) Students compare answers.
6) Students write a two-paragraph summary of the article.

Lesson Plan #2

Class:	Upper Intermediate Listening	Week 3
Aims:	to practice listening to an authentic news broadcast and to get key information from it	

Resources: tape recorder; tape; worksheet

Activities:

1) Ask students to work in groups and list five important events in the news in the last week.
2) Groups share information.
3) Play the tape. Students decide if any of the events
   they mentioned are talked about on the tape.
4) Distribute the worksheet, which lists three topics
   and a set of questions. Students listen for answers
   to the questions.
5) Students compare their answers in groups.
6) Play the tape again. Discuss problems students
   had with any words or expressions on the tape.

In lesson plan #1, the reading lesson, the teacher divides the lesson into six activities which focus on prediction, reading for global comprehension, reading for detailed comprehension, giving and getting feedback, and summarizing. In lesson plan #2, the listening lesson, the teacher similarly divides the lesson into six activities which focus on gathering background information, listening for key words, listening for specific information, giving and getting feedback, and diagnosing listening difficulties. Despite the many kinds of activities which teachers use in language teaching, a limited number of activity types tend to recur no matter what kind of approach or methodology the teacher is using. These activity types can be classified according to the following categories.

Presentation activities. These are tasks in which new learning material is presented for the first time. A presentation activity serves to introduce and clarify a new learning item. This could be a lexical item, a grammatical item, a function, a discourse feature, or a learning strategy. For example, a teacher may present patterns with "if clauses" using a chart or table as the first activity in a grammar lesson. Not all lessons include a presentation activity. For example, in the listening lesson plan there is no direct presentation of the strategies. A different lesson plan for the same lesson might have included the teacher first talking about listening strategies and which strategies to use when listening to a news broadcast.

Practice activities. These are defined as tasks which involve performance or learning of an item that has been previously presented. Practice activities in language teaching often involve a degree of control over student performance or involve the use of a model. For example, in a conversation lesson, dialogues may be used to practice sentence patterns, grammar, or functions, and drills may be used to practice pronunciation and to develop sentence fluency. In the reading lesson plan, most of the lesson is devoted to activities which practice reading skills.

Memorization activities. These tasks involve memorization of information or learning material. Memorization activities may be used as a strategy to help consolidate new learning items or as preparation for a subsequent activity. For example, students may be asked to memorize a list of vocabulary which they will later use in a speaking task. While traditional approaches to language teaching (e.g., Grammar Translation and the Audiolingual Method) made extensive use of memorization activities, contemporary approaches tend to discourage memorization in favor of activities which promote more creative uses of language.

Comprehension activities. These tasks require students to develop or demonstrate their understanding of written or spoken texts. Comprehension activities may address different levels of comprehension, including literal comprehension (understanding meanings stated explicitly in a text), inferential comprehension (drawing conclusions and making predictions based on information in the text), and evaluation (making judgments about the content of a text based on personal or other values). For example, students may read a passage and make inferences about the author's attitude toward the topic or listen to a lecture and write a summary of it. Several activities in the reading and listening classes above focus on comprehension skills.

Application activities. These are defined as tasks which require learners to use in a creative way knowledge or skills that have been previously presented and practiced. Application activities may require students to integrate knowledge and skills acquired from different sources, to apply learned items to a new context or situation, or to personalize learning items through relating them to their own ideas, needs, feelings, and experiences. For example, after having practiced a dialogue in which certain sentence patterns or functions were used, students may now perform a role play in which they have to use the patterns and functions creatively in a situation involving transfer and negotiation of meaning. An application activity in a writing class might represent the final stage in a sequence of activities in which students first read an essay where certain rhetorical forms are used (presentation), do a set of exercises to practice using different rhetorical and discourse devices in paragraphs (practice), and then complete a written assignment incorporating the rhetorical and discourse devices using ideas and information of their own.

Strategy activities. These tasks develop particular learning strategies and approaches to learning. For example, in order to improve learners' use of systematic guessing when encountering new vocabulary in a reading text, learners may be given exercises which train them to focus on suffixes, prefixes, and word order as useful linguistic clues for guessing the meanings of new words in a text. In listening, learners may be trained to use clues in the situation to help understand meanings. This could involve, for example, making predictions based on the setting, on the roles of the people involved in the interaction, and on the people's intentions and purposes. In the reading lesson (lesson plan #1), the first activity, which involved making predictions based on the headline of a newspaper article, was designed to develop the strategy of using predictions to guide one's reading.

Affective activities. These include tasks which have no specific language learning goal but are intended to improve the motivational climate of the classroom and to develop the students' interest, confidence, and positive attitudes toward learning. For example, in a foreign language class, students may keep a journal in which they write about their feelings, fears, and satisfactions in relation to the experiences they have in the class. They may share these both with their classmates and the teacher, and attempt to resolve concerns as they arise.

Feedback activities. These tasks are used to give feedback on learning or on some aspect of performance on the activity. For example, in a writing lesson, after completing a first draft of their assignment, students may work in pairs to read each other's assignments and provide suggestions for improvement. This feedback may address content, organization, or clarity of expression, and serves to provide information that may be useful to the student when revising the piece of writing. In the listening lesson (lesson plan #2), the teacher used a feedback activity when playing the tape at the end of the lesson and discussed problems students had with any words or expressions on the tape.

Assessment activities. These tasks enable the teacher or learner to evaluate the extent to which the goals of an activity or lesson have been successfully accomplished. These activities may be used to diagnose areas which need further teaching or to evaluate student performance.

Tests of different kinds are common examples of assessment activities; however, most classroom activities can also be used for assessment if they are used to determine how much students have learned rather than as a presentation, practice, or an application activity.

This classification is intended to help focus on the relationship between activity types and the purposes for which they are used in language teaching. Such a classification cannot be regarded as definitive, since some activities can be used for several different purposes, and distinctions between activity types can overlap. However, such a list can be useful in trying to clarify what it is that teachers do when they teach and why they select the kind of classroom activities that they commonly use.

Ideally the activities selected by the teacher are appropriate to the purposes for which they are intended, but sometimes there is a mismatch between activities and purposes, as in the following examples taken from a supervisor's comments on two student teachers' lessons:

In your reading class, your reported goals were to develop fluency in reading and to develop good reading habits, including reading for main ideas and keeping the purpose of the passage in mind while reading. This should involve a top-down approach to reading, i.e., one in which the reader is encouraged to use background information, prediction, and context while reading, rather than to use a word-by-word reading strategy. However, you use reading aloud as a regular classroom activity. There is a conflict here between teaching goals and the activity used to support these goals, since reading aloud requires students to focus on the form of a text rather than its meaning and to give every word in the text equal importance.

You report that your goals in your writing class are to develop fluency in writing and to develop the student's ability to use drafting and revision skills when writing. However, the classroom activities you most commonly use involve copying and making minor changes to model paragraphs and compositions and sentence-based exercises which give students little opportunity for drafting and revision.

Discussion

1. The following activities are commonly used in language classrooms. What kinds of activities are they according to the classification in this section?

a. *Dictation.* The teacher reads aloud a paragraph sentence by sentence, and gives students time to write it down.
b. *Cloze passage.* Students are given a passage where every sixth or seventh word is missing and they try to complete the missing words.
c. *Dialogue reading.* Students are given the script of a dialogue, they learn it and act it out in front of the class.
d. *Dictionary training.* Students are taught how to use a learner's dictionary.
e. *Brainstorming.* Students think of as many ideas as they can related to a topic before beginning to write about it.
f. *Grammar rules.* Students read a handout explaining the difference between the past tense and the simple past continuous.
g. *Debate.* Students take part in a class debate.
h. *Songs.* Students learn songs in the target language culture.
i. *Problem sharing.* Students role-play a difficult experience they had when they tried to use the language with a native speaker.
j. *Reading aloud.* Students read a passage aloud in front of the class.
2. If you are teaching a class, discuss your approach to teaching with a teacher who teaches a class similar to yours. What kinds of activities do you use most often in your teaching? How would you classify them on the list in this section? Do you use any activities that cannot easily be classified on the list? How would you describe such activities? What purposes do you use them for? If you are observing a class, what kinds of activities does the teacher most often use?

Dimensions of language learning activities

In selecting and designing classroom activities to accomplish specific teaching and learning goals, a number of issues have to be resolved. These relate to the following dimensions of activities: purpose, procedures, sequencing, complexity, resources, grouping, strategies, language, timing, outcomes, and assessment.

How will the purposes of an activity be communicated to the students? A number of options are available in introducing the purposes of an activity. For example, the teacher may ask students to begin an activity without explaining its purpose, or the teacher may decide to explain why he or she is using a particular activity. Some activities are very familiar to students, and teachers often assign them without explaining what their purpose is. Dictation, group discussion, and oral drills are examples of such activities. At other times the teacher may choose a particular strategy to communicate the goals of an activity or to introduce the activity. Such strategies include:

- Saying that students will enjoy the activity.
- Saying that students will benefit from the activity.
- Describing what students will learn from the activity.
- Saying how the activity will prepare students for a test.
- Saying how the activity relates to previous or later learning.
- Asking students to do the activity and, after they have completed it, asking them what they thought the purpose of the activity was.

What procedures will students use in completing an activity?   For most classroom activities a number of options are available. For example, if students are asked to write a short composition, should they gather information and take notes and then prepare a first draft, or should they go straight into a first draft? When reading a magazine article, should they preview the article first by skimming through it quickly, or should they begin by reading the article carefully? The extent to which students are clear on the procedures they are to use in carrying out an activity will affect both how quickly they understand the dimensions of the activity and the effectiveness with which they complete it. Strategies used to communicate procedures for completing an activity include:

- Describing the procedures the students should use.
- Demonstrating the procedures in front of the class.
- Selecting a student to demonstrate the procedure.
- Leaving students to work out their own procedures and then discussing the effectiveness of the procedures they use.

How will the activity be sequenced in relation to other activities within the same lesson?   We saw in Chapter 6 that sequencing decisions reflect either the specific assumptions underlying a methodology (e.g., that pre-communicative activities normally precede communicative activities in lessons based on Communicative Language Teaching) or the formats for lessons that individual teachers develop through experience. Issues related to sequencing of activities are discussed in Chapter 6 and need not be restated here.

What kinds of demands does the activity make on learn-ers? Tikunoff (1985b) identifies four dimensions of task complexity – risk, ambiguity, knowledge, and procedure.

Risk: Low-risk tasks are those with which students are relatively familiar; they know what is expected of them.

Ambiguity: Ambiguous tasks are those in which there is no single,
straightforward interpretation, or in which multiple interpretations
are possible.

Knowledge: The knowledge demands of a task depend on the extent to
which the task involves lower or higher cognitive levels. Tikunoff
(1985b) suggests that memory tasks are at a relatively low cognitive
level, problem-solving tasks are at a relatively mid-cognitive level,
and tasks which requires students to be innovative, creative, and in-
ventive are at a high cognitive level.

Procedure: The difficulty of a task may also depend on how it is to be
carried out. Tasks with low-level procedural demands involve simple sequential operations. A task with higher-level procedural
demands requires the student to perform several operations at the
same time, such as making an oral presentation before the class on
an assigned topic without the use of notes.

What resources will be required? Activities differ in the kind of resources that are needed to support them. For example, with activities in a composition class, the resources students need to use may include a file of articles to read to gather information about the topic; sample composi-tions on the topic to illustrate various rhetorical models; a revision checklist which draws students' attention to specific features of sentence, paragraph, or text organization that they should attend to in revising; a set of revision questions which students ask themselves about the first draft of their compositions as a preparation for revision activities. Re-sources may include textbooks or teacher-produced materials. Both kinds of materials may be selected to accommodate different learning ap-proaches, student interests, and proficiency levels within the same class.

What grouping arrangements will be used? A central question in planning learning activities is deciding whether students will complete them individually, in pairs, in groups, or as a whole-class activity (see Chapter 7). Grouping arrangements should be maximally effective ac-cording to the particular type of activity which has been chosen. The decision about what grouping arrangement to choose may be based on a number of factors:

Pedagogical factors. A pair or group activity might be considered essential for a speaking task, but not necessarily for a listening task.

Ability levels. In setting up groups, decisions must be made as to
whether students of mixed ability or of similar abilities should form
a group.

The teacher's personality and individual teaching style. Some teachers
like to be in control of a lesson, for example, and hence make use
of whole-class learning arrangements.

The teacher's personal philosophy of teaching. A teacher may feel that
students learn best when working with others and that the teacher's
role is that of facilitator.

The institutional culture. Some teaching institutions may favor particular learning arrangements. An institution that favors collaborative
learning, for example, is likely to encourage teachers to use group
work.

Cultural factors. In some cultures students expect the teacher to be in
charge of the class and do not think they can learn anything useful
from working with other students.

*Should a particular learning strategy be used in carrying out an
activity?*   For any particular learning activity, the teacher often has to
decide which strategy is likely to be most effective (see Chapter 3). For
example, in completing a reading comprehension activity where students
read a text in order to answer questions about it, several strategies are
available. Students could (a) first read the comprehension questions at
the end of the passage and then skim the passage for answers; (b) first
read the comprehension questions and then read the article carefully for
the answers; (c) first read the passage carefully, read the questions, and
then skim for the answers; or, (d) first skim the entire article, read the
comprehension questions, and then read the article carefully for the
answers. The teacher must decide which of these strategies to encourage
students to use.

*What language or language learning focus should the activity
have?*   Learning activities vary in their goals. For example, an activity
may focus on a specific area of language such as developing particular
skills or practicing an item of grammar, a feature of pronunciation, or
vocabulary, or the activity may encourage the integrated use of a variety
of aspects of language. An activity may focus on accuracy, appropriate
language, or fluency. The design of learning activities and the way they
are introduced and presented in class are key factors in focusing learners'
attention on the linguistic dimensions of the task and the language

resources they may need to use in completing it. For example, before introducing a role-play activity in which students will practice giving invitations and accepting or declining them, the teacher must decide whether the activity will include a focus on specific ways of inviting, and hence pre-teach some of the language the students will need, or whether the students will use their own linguistic resources in carrying out the role play (see Chapter 9 for further discussion of this issue).

How much time should students spend on the activity?   The amount of time students spend on classroom activities has been identified as one of the most important factors affecting student learning (Brophy and Good 1986; Fisher et al. 1978). Three aspects of this issue have been identified:

- The amount of time that has been allowed by the teacher; this is known as *allocated time.*
- The degree to which students are engaged in the activity during the time provided; this is known as *time-on-task.*
- The extent to which students are successfully engaged: that is, the proportion of time-on-task during which students are achieving high accuracy in completing the activity; this is known as *academic learning time.*

Teachers vary in the amount of academic learning time that they manage to achieve within their lessons. For example, during a 50 minute lesson, only 30–35 minutes may actually be used for instruction (allocated time), and the proportion of that time which can be regarded as academic learning time may be much less. An important challenge for teachers is to maximize academic learning time within lessons – the time students spend involved in learning activities and succeeding with them – which is the most important variable affecting students' achievement (Levin with Long 1981).

What will the outcome of the activity be?   Activities vary in the extent to which they lead to a particular learning outcome or product. For some activities, doing the activity itself is the main learning goal; the focus is more on the processes involved than on any particular learning outcome. Examples of activities of this kind include pleasure reading and free conversation. For other activities, however, particular learner outcomes, such as book reports or term papers, may be required. Teachers hence have to consider questions such as the following:

- Will there be a learning outcome for the activity?

- Will all students be expected to produce the same outcome?
- Will students have any choice in the kind of learning outcome they are expected to produce?

How will student performance on the activity be assessed? Not all classroom activities lead to assessment of student performance (e.g., presentation and affective activities); however, assessment decisions are involved in planning some classroom activities. These involve consideration of the following factors:

The focus of assessment. What is being assessed – for example, the product the student has produced or the student's participation in the activity?

The recipient of the assessment. Who will be evaluated – for example, individual students, groups of students, or the whole class?

The setting of the assessment. Where will assessment information be given – for example, publicly so that everyone can hear it, or privately for each individual recipient?

The form of assessment. How will the activity be assessed – for example, will a formal assessment procedure be used, or will the teacher assess the activity informally?

The consequences of assessment. What will be done with the assessment information – for example, if student performance on an activity is not at a satisfactory level of accuracy, will the teacher spend time on remedial grammar exercises or give the students another activity on a different topic covering the same teaching points?

For both teachers and learners the concept of learning activity is a central one, since most language lessons are organized around the completion of activities of one kind or another. Learning how to select and use learning activities effectively hence requires both an awareness of what different kinds of activities are good for, as well as recognition of the factors which need to be considered when using activities in the language classroom.

Discussion

1. What are your criteria for determining the success of a learning activity? What features do you think an effective learning activity should include? Discuss this in relation to a specific class or lesson you are teaching or observing.

2. How important do you think it is to explain the purpose of a language learning activity to students? Give reasons to support your answers.
3. With a partner, discuss the strategies for communicating procedures for completing an activity described on page 168. Think of a particular learning activity you are familiar with. Which strategies would you normally use? Now select another option on the list and consider its advantages and disadvantages.
4. What grouping arrangements do you typically use or expect to use in teaching? Do you think a teacher should vary grouping arrangements regularly? What factors influence choice of grouping arrangements?
5. Review the ten dimensions of activities presented in this chapter. Which ones do you think should normally be considered in planning lessons? What other dimensions of activities do you think are important?

Follow-up activities

Analyzing learning activities

1. Identify learning goals for the following activities:
   a. Students are given a copy of a dialogue. They listen to the dialogue and mark which words are stressed.
   b. Students listen to a description of a person and identify the correct person by selecting from among five pictures.
   c. Students work in pairs and look at similar but slightly different pictures. Student A describes picture 1 to his or her partner, and the partner identifies any differences in picture 2.
   d. Students are given twenty sentences in random order and decide in groups the best way to reorder them to make a story.
   e. Each student in the class is given one sentence which forms part of a story. One student reads aloud his or her sentence; others try to figure out whether their sentence goes before or after it. Gradually they reconstruct the story.
   f. Students are given thirty verbs and are asked to arrange them into categories of their choice.
2. Suggest language learning activities to attain these goals:
   a. To teach students the principle of sentence focus – that is, that different words in a sentence can be given stronger stress according to the focus of information in the sentence.

  b. To teach students how to write paragraphs containing topic
     sentences.
  c. To teach students to use effective note-taking strategies when
     listening to lectures.
  d. To train students to hear the difference between words beginning
     with /sh/ and /s/.
  e. To practice using the present continuous to describe ongoing
     events.
  f. To practice job interview skills.
3. Examine the examples from EFL textbooks on pages 175–177.
   What is the purpose of each activity in the extracts? Classify the
   activities into the following categories:
   a. presentation activity
   b. practice activity
   c. memorization activity
   d. comprehension activity
   e. application activity
   f. strategy activity
   g. affective activity
   h. feedback activity
   i. assessment activity

Journal activity

In your journal this week, describe some of the activities you used or
observed in teaching. Why were these particular activities used? How did
they relate to the goals of the course? To what degree do you think a
match between the activities and the intended purposes was achieved?

Recording task

Record a lesson by placing a cassette recorder on your (or the teacher's)
desk. Then review the recording and calculate how much of the lesson
was allocated time – that is, time actually spent on learning, as opposed
to noninstructional time allocated to such procedural matters as roll call
and announcements.

Classroom observation task

Observe a language lesson and focus on one particular student, or a pair,
or a small group of students working together. Approximately how

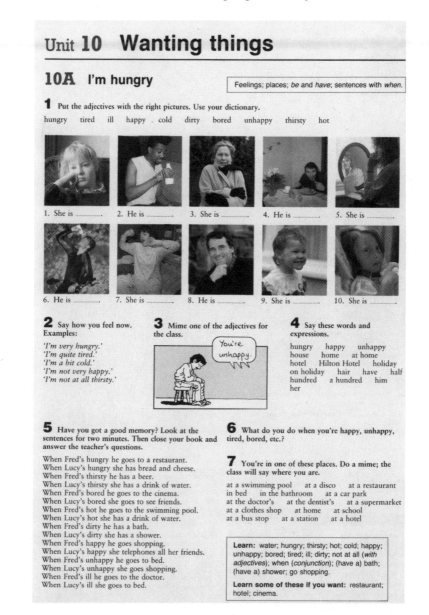

Extract 1.   (Reprinted with permission from M. Swan and C. Walter, 1990, *The New Cambridge English Course*, p. 48, published by Cambridge University Press.)

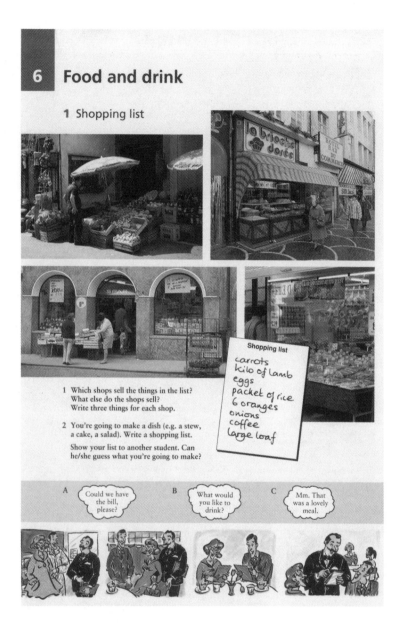

Extract 2.   (Reprinted with permission from A. Doff and C. Jones, 1991, *Language in Use: A Pre-intermediate Course,* pp. 28–9, published by Cambridge University Press.)

2 National dishes

1 Read these descriptions of Korean dishes, and match them with the pictures.
Which *two* would you choose?

1 *Oi-naengch'ae*

Oi-naengch'ae is a kind of soup. It is made from cucumbers and onions, and it also has sugar and vinegar in it. You eat it cold.

2 *Paeksolgi*

For this dish you need rice, beans and sugar. You cook the rice and beans and make them into a kind of cake. You serve it cold with fruit.

3 *Poggumbap*

Poggumbap is a rice dish which is very popular in Korea. The rice is fried with small pieces of crab and pork. It is served hot.

4 *Pindaeddok*

These are Korean pancakes. They are made from beans and flour, and also have meat and cabbage in them. You can eat them hot or cold.

5 *Shinsollo*

This is a kind of stew. It is made from different kinds of meat cooked with vegetables, nuts and spices. You serve it in a large pot which you put in the middle of the table.

2 You're planning a special meal for some foreign visitors. Write a menu and include
– a starter
– a main course
– a dessert
– drinks

Explain to your guests what each dish is.

3 Eating out

1 What's happening in the pictures below? Put the remarks in the right order.

[▭] Now listen to the tape and check your answers.

2 Work in threes. Act out a scene in a restaurant.

D   I'll have the chicken, please.

E   Have you reserved a table?

F   Are you ready to order now?

G   What about this table by the window?

Extract 2.   (*continued*)

much of the time did the student(s) spend "on-task" – that is, how much of the time was the student actually engaged in completing the activity?

Lesson-report tasks

1. For a lesson you teach, first identify the purpose for which you use the activities in the lesson in as much detail as possible. When you teach the lesson, say as little as possible about the purpose of the activities you assign. At the end of the lesson, give out a brief report sheet listing each activity the students complete. Ask the students to identify the purpose of each activity. How similar were the students' descriptions of purposes to yours?
2. Use the lesson-report form in Appendix 1 to monitor the activity types used over a two-week period. How much variety is there in the activity types you use? For what purposes did you use these activities? Compare the information you collect with another teacher's self-report information.

Action research case study #6

Student performance on learning activities

This project was conducted by a teacher at a language institute in an ESL context.

INITIAL REFECTION

I teach a group of students who are preparing to attend an American university. I feel they learn best when they have a chance to practice English using group work activities which encourage free production of the language and learner–learner interaction. I often use problem-solving discussions in my lessons to provide such practice. I wanted to know, however, what happens when my students carry out such communicative tasks when their production is unmonitored by the teacher. In particular I wanted to investigate the fluency, accuracy, and appropriateness of student language use when they engaged in problem-solving discussions. I used the following questions to guide this project:

1. How accurate is student production during discussion activities?
2. How fluent is student production during discussion activities?
3. How appropriate is student production during discussion activities?

PLANNING

I decided to audio-record student discussions as they were completing a problem-solving activity and then analyze the language that they used. The activity I decided to use was "The Plane Crash," a situation where an airplane will soon crash, with twenty passengers but only ten parachutes. The students discuss the problem in groups of five, and have to agree on which ten individuals on the plane should survive.

ACTION

I brought four tape recorders into the class and gave one to each group. I had to make sure that the groups were well spaced and that the students spoke into the microphones. I gave the students a handout and explained the activity to them. The students understood what to do and immediately began their discussions. The activity lasted for about 20 minutes. Later, I took the tapes home and listened to them. I checked the accuracy of student production by counting the number of lexical errors and grammatical errors. To determine students' fluency I calculated the total amount of speech for each student and the number of hesitations. To judge the appropriateness of student language I looked at the way students expressed agreement and disagreement. I made a chart for each student which I completed as I listened to the tapes and coded the data.

OBSERVATION

I was impressed with the overall quality of student language as they carried out their problem-solving activity. There was a high degree of interaction among the students, with each individual taking part in the discussion. I noticed from the data that students were more fluent than I had thought; they were able to keep the conversation going without any sustained hesitation, pauses, or breakdowns. The students were also relatively accurate in their speech and when errors did occur, they were often able to self-correct. There were few errors that resulted in miscommunication; most of the errors were in the use of articles and prepositions. I was less pleased, however, with the appropriateness of the language for agreeing and disagreeing. The students were very direct with each other, using language such as "No, you're wrong" where a less direct form of expressing disagreement would have been more polite.

REFLECTION

This project was useful in determining how my students perform on a specific type of activity. The results confirmed my beliefs about the usefulness of problem-solving discussions as practice activities. I am encouraged by my students' abilities to speak English, but realize that I need to teach my students politeness strategies using more indirect language.

Appendix: Lesson-report form for activity types

CLASS _____   DATE _____
GOALS AND CONTENT OF LESSON _____

Activities Used in the Lesson	Type of Activity	Time Spent on the Activity	Purpose of Activity
EXAMPLE: *Assigned word study exercise in the workbook*	*Practice activity*	*10 minutes*	*To consolidate students' use of new vocabulary*

9 *Language use in the classroom*

One distinguishing feature of language classrooms is that language is usually both the goal of the lesson and the means by which this goal is achieved. The teacher has a number of competing concerns. For example, the teacher plans activities designed to facilitate the learners' acquisition and use of the target language. At the same time, however, the teacher uses the target language as the principal means for giving instructions and directions, modeling target language patterns, and giving feedback on student performance. The students likewise learn language both in order to negotiate classroom interaction with the teacher and other students, and to complete the demands of classroom work. This chapter focuses on the linguistic dimensions of these processes and their effects on the kind of language use that occurs in second and foreign language classrooms. The chapter examines in particular (1) how teachers modify their language, (2) how teachers use questions, (3) how teachers give feedback, and (4) the language of classroom interaction, including the language students use when completing activities.

How teachers modify their language

A major portion of class time in teaching is taken up by teachers talking in front of the class (see Chapter 7). No matter what teaching strategies or methods a teacher uses, it is necessary to give directions, explain activities, clarify the procedures students should use on an activity, and check students' understanding.

A large proportion of the teacher's total communicative efforts can be taken up with coaxing along the communicative process itself, especially when the learners are relative beginners. The teacher has to get the pupils' attention, monitor their understanding by constant checking, clarify, explain, define and when appropriate summarise.   (Ellis 1984: 120)

This is seen in the following examples of a teacher explaining a textbook exercise to students and monitoring the students' progress.

T: Have you finished yet? Have you completed the questions at the bottom of the page?

S1: Not yet.

T: [*to another student*] Where are you up to, Juan? Are you finished yet?

S2: No, not yet.

T: Try to finish up to here [*points at book*].

T: Write your answers on a separate piece of paper, Akito, don't do it in your book.

T: You work together with Akito now and check your answers. Do you understand?

S3: OK. Check answers.

T: Yes. Check your answers. You and Akito check your answers together.

The repetitive nature of the teacher's requests and instructions in this example is characteristic of what happens in teaching. Repetition is one of many strategies teachers use to make their directions and instructions understandable to the learners. Other strategies (Chaudron 1988) include:

Speaking more slowly. When teachers speak to language learners in the classroom, they often use a slower rate of speech than they would use in other situations.

Using pauses. Teachers tend to pause more and to use longer pauses when teaching language learners, particularly lower-level students. These pauses give learners more time to process what the teacher has said and hence facilitate their comprehension.

Changing pronunciation. Teachers may sometimes use a clearer articulation or a more standard style of speech, one which contains fewer reductions and contractions than they would use outside of a teaching situation. For example, instead of saying, "Couldja read that line, Juan?" the teacher might more carefully enunciate "Could you . . . ?"

Modifying vocabulary. Teachers often replace a difficult word with what they think is a more commonly used word. For example, the teacher might ask, "What do you think this picture *shows*?" instead of "What do you think this picture *depicts*?" However, teachers sometimes unwittingly "complicate" vocabulary instead of simplifying it. For example, teachers might say, "What do you think this picture is *about*?" supplying an idiomatic (but not necessarily simpler) replacement for *depicts.*

Modifying grammar. Language teachers often simplify the grammatical structure of sentences in the classroom. For example, teachers may use fewer subordinate clauses in a classroom situation than in other contexts, or avoid using complex tenses.

Modifying discourse. Teachers may repeat themselves or answer their own questions in order to make themselves understood, as we saw in the dialogue earlier.

These kinds of modifications in teachers' speech can lead to a special type of discourse which has been referred to as *teacher talk.* When teachers use teacher talk they are trying to make themselves as easy to understand as possible, and effective teacher talk may provide essential support to facilitate both language comprehension and learner production. Krashen (1985) argues that this is how teachers provide learners with "comprehensible input" (input which is finely tuned to the learner's level of comprehension), which he sees as "the essential ingredient for second language acquisition" (p. 4). However, sometimes teachers may develop a variety of teacher talk which would not sound natural outside of the classroom. The following are examples of teachers using this variety of teacher talk when teaching low-level ESL learners.

In your house, you . . . a tub . . . you (gestures) *wash.* (The teacher is explaining the meaning of "wash.")

I want to speak another person. He not here. What good thing for say now? (The teacher is explaining how to take telephone messages.)

Not other students listen. I no want. Necessary you speak. Maybe I say what is your name. The writing not important. (The teacher is explaining an interview procedure.)

The book . . . we have . . . (holds up book) . . . book is necessary for class. Right . . . necessary for school. You have book. (The teacher is reminding the students to bring their books to class.)

Although these examples may be extreme, they illustrate that in their efforts to provide students with comprehensible input, teachers may sometimes develop a style of speaking that does not reflect natural speech.

Discussion

1. Review the list of strategies for modifying teacher talk on pages 183–184. Which of these strategies do you (or the teacher you are observing) use most when teaching? Which of these strategies are most helpful for the learners?
2. To what extent do you think teachers should modify their language when teaching? What are some of the advantages and disadvantages of such modification?
3. How can teachers avoid overusing teacher talk or using an especially unnatural variety of it?

Teachers' questions

Research suggests that questioning is one of the most common techniques used by teachers. In some classrooms over half of class time is taken up with question-and-answer exchanges (Gall 1984). There are several reasons why questions are so commonly used in teaching.

- They stimulate and maintain students' interest.
- They encourage students to think and focus on the content of the lesson.
- They enable a teacher to clarify what a student has said.
- They enable a teacher to elicit particular structures or vocabulary items.
- They enable teachers to check students' understanding.
- They encourage student participation in a lesson.

Second language researchers have also examined the contribution of teachers' questions to classroom second language learning. They have proposed that the questions play a crucial role in language acquisition: "They can be used to allow the learner to keep participating in the discourse and even modify it so that the language used becomes more comprehensible and personally relevant" (Banbrook and Skehan 1989: 142).

Types of teacher questions

There are many different ways to classify questions (Mehan 1979; Sinclair and Brazil 1982; White and Lightbown 1984), and as researchers have observed it is sometimes difficult to arrive at discrete and directly observable categories (Banbrook and Skehan 1989). For the purposes of examining the role of questions in the classroom, three kinds of questions are distinguished here – procedural, convergent, and divergent.

Procedural questions Procedural questions have to do with classroom procedures and routines, and classroom management, as opposed to the content of learning. For example, the following questions occurred in classrooms while teachers were checking that assignments had been completed, that instructions for a task were clear, and that students were ready for a new task.

Did everyone bring their homework?
Do you all understand what I want you to do?
How much more time do you need?
Can you all read what I've written on the blackboard?
Did anyone bring a dictionary to class?
Why aren't you doing the assignment?

Procedural questions have a different function from questions designed to help students master the content of a lesson. Many of the questions teachers ask are designed to engage students in the content of the lesson, to facilitate their comprehension, and to promote classroom interaction. These questions can be classified into two types – convergent questions and divergent questions, depending on the kind of answer they are intended to elicit (Kindsvatter, Willen, and Ishler 1988).

Convergent questions Convergent questions encourage similar student responses, or responses which focus on a central theme. These responses are often short answers, such as "yes" or "no" or short statements. They do not usually require students to engage in higher-level thinking in order to come up with a response but often focus on the recall of previously presented information. Language teachers often ask a rapid sequence of convergent questions to help develop aural skills and vocabulary and to encourage whole-class participation before moving on to some other teaching technique (see Chapter 7). For example, the following questions were used by a teacher in introducing a reading lesson focusing on the effects of computers on everyday life. Before the teacher began the lesson she led students into the topic of the reading by asking the following convergent questions:

How many of you have a personal computer in your home?
Do you use it every day?
What do you mainly use it for?
What are some other machines that you have in your home?

What are the names of some computer companies?
What is the difference between software and hardware?

Divergent questions Divergent questions are the opposite of convergent questions. They encourage diverse student responses which are not short answers and which require students to engage in higher-level thinking. They encourage students to provide their own information rather than to recall previously presented information. For example, after asking the convergent questions above, the teacher went on to ask divergent questions such as the following:

How have computers had an economic impact on society?
How would businesses today function without computers?
Do you think computers have had any negative effects on society?
What are the best ways of promoting the use of computers in
    education?

Questioning skills

In view of the importance of questioning as a teaching strategy, the skill with which teachers use questions has received a considerable amount of attention in teacher education. Among the issues that have been identified are the following.

The range of question types teachers use. It has often been observed that teachers tend to ask more convergent than divergent questions. These questions serve to facilitate the recall of information rather than to generate student ideas and classroom communication. Since convergent questions require short answers, they may likewise provide limited opportunities for students to produce and practice the target language. Long and Sato (1983) compared the number of "display questions" (questions that teachers know the answer to and which are designed to elicit or display particular structures) and "referential questions" (questions that teachers do not know the answers to) in naturalistic and classroom discourse. They found that in naturalistic discourse referential questions are more frequent than display questions, whereas display questions are much more frequent in whole-class teaching in ESL classrooms.

Student participation. In many classrooms, students have few opportunities to ask questions on their own, although they may be given the opportunity to answer questions. Even when teachers give students opportunities to ask and answer questions, they may address their questions to only a few of the students in the class – those lying within their action zone (see Chapter 7). Jackson and Lahaderne (1967) found that some students are twenty-five times more likely to be called on to speak in a class than others. In language classrooms, where students may be of different levels of ability, the fact that some students have much more difficulty answering questions than others may lead the teacher to call on only those students in the class who can be relied upon to answer the question in order to maintain the momentum of the class. This reinforces the teacher's tendency to direct questions to only certain students in the class.

Wait-time. An important dimension of a teacher's questioning skills is *wait-time,* that is, the length of time the teacher waits after asking the question before calling on a student to answer it, rephrasing the question, directing the question to another student, or giving the answer (Rowe 1974, cited in Kindsvatter et al. 1988). Teachers often use a very short wait-time (e.g., one second), which is rarely sufficient to enable students to respond. When wait-time is increased to three to five seconds, the amount of student participation as well as the quality of that participation often increases (Long et al. 1984).

Discussion

1. Under what circumstances is using convergent questions an effective questioning strategy in a language class? When are such questions likely to be less effective? How can teachers ensure that they ask a balance of convergent and divergent questions during lessons?
2. What are several different ways in which teachers can monitor their questioning skills? Discuss the advantages and disadvantages of each method.

Feedback

Providing feedback to learners on their performance is another important aspect of teaching. Feedback can be either positive or negative and may serve not only to let learners know how well they have performed but also to increase motivation and build a supportive classroom climate. In language classrooms, feedback on a student's spoken language may be a response either to the content of what a student has produced or to the form of an utterance.

Feedback on content

A variety of strategies is available in giving feedback on content. For example:

Acknowledging a correct answer. The teacher acknowledges that a student's answer is correct by saying, for example, "Good," "Yes, that's right," or "Fine."

Indicating an incorrect answer. The teacher indicates that a student's answer is incorrect by saying, for example, "No, that's not quite right," or "Mmm."

Praising. The teacher compliments a student for an answer, for example, by saying "Yes, an excellent answer."

Expanding or modifying a student's answer. The teacher responds to a vague or incomplete answer by providing more information, or rephrasing the answer in the teacher's own words. For example:

T: Does anyone know the capital of the United States?
S: Washington.
T: Yes, Washington, D.C. That's located on the east coast.

Repeating. The teacher repeats the student's answer.

Summarizing. The teacher gives a summary of what a student or group of students has said.

Criticizing. The teacher criticizes a student for the kind of response provided. For example:

T: Raymond, can you point out the topic sentence in this paragraph?
R: The first sentence.
T: How can it be the first sentence? Remember, I said the first sentence is not always the topic sentence in every paragraph. Look again!

Feedback on form

In language classrooms, feedback is often directed toward the accuracy of what a student says. A number of issues are involved in error feedback. These include decisions about (1) whether learner errors should be corrected, (2) which kinds of learner errors should be corrected, and (3) how learner errors should be corrected (Hendrickson 1978).

Learners and teachers often have different preferences concerning error correction. Nunan (1988) reports that adult learners in Australia viewed error correction as very important, whereas their teachers did not value it as highly. Similar findings have been found elsewhere (Chaudron 1988).

Studies of which errors teachers tend to correct show that teachers are most likely to correct content errors, followed by vocabulary errors, and errors of grammar or pronunciation (Chaudron 1988).

The issue of how learner errors should be corrected has been a focus of considerable discussion in language teaching (Harmer 1991; Omaggio 1986). Feedback on form can be accomplished in different ways, such as:

- Asking the student to repeat what he or she said.
- Pointing out the error and asking the student to self-correct.
- Commenting on an error and explaining why it is wrong, without having the student repeat the correct form.
- Asking another student to correct the error.
- Using a gesture to indicate that an error has been made.

The following example illustrates the different kinds of feedback teachers give during classroom interaction. The teacher is questioning students about when they began their studies.

T	When did you start? [nominates by gesture]
S4	I start in Excess since the eleventh of January.
T	When did you arrive? You arrived on the eleventh of January, did you? You must have started the next day, did you?
S2	The eleventh of January
S5	No, I we start at thirteenth
T	On the thirteenth of January. When did you start at Essex? [nominates by gesture]
S1	I start at Essex on the thirteenth of January.
T	On the thirteenth of January.
S1	Yes
T	Again.
S1	I start at Essex on the thirteenth of January.
T	Eulyces [pause]
	I started
S2	I stotted
T	Started
S1	Start
S2	I . . . ( ) [aside to S1 in Spanish] I start on on Essess eh fourteen of January
T	I
S2	Fourteenth January
T	I started at Essex on the thirteenth of January. All right Eulyces: on the thirteenth of January . . .
S2	On the th–

T	Thirteenth
S2	On the fourteenth of January
T	Of January
S2	Of January
T	On the thirteenth of January
S2	On fourteenth of January
T	All together . . . on the thirteenth
SSS	On the thirteenth of January
T	All right. I started at Essex [gestures for choral response]
SSS	I started at Essex on the thirteenth of January.
T	Good. Good. Were you at university before?

(Allwright 1975: 108–9)

In this extract, the teacher corrects both the form and the content of what the learners say. In the beginning of the extract, the teacher ignores grammatical errors but picks up the factual error concerning the date. After the learners sort out the correct date the teacher provides a model of the correct phrase. In the next utterance, the learner makes an error in verb tense form. The teacher ignores this error, confirms the correct date, and then asks the learner to repeat. The verb tense error occurs again and the teacher calls on a different student. The student hesitates and the teacher models the beginning of the sentence with the correct verb tense. The learner makes an error in pronunciation, which the teacher corrects by modeling the correct form. However, the student, after consulting another student in Spanish, repeats another student's error rather than using the form provided by the teacher. The teacher remodels the sentence, seems to realize S2's difficulties, and then remodels the final phrase. At the end of the extract, the teacher transfers the error treatment to the whole class through choral repetition.

Allwright (1975) observes that teachers often give imprecise feedback on learner errors. Rather than showing the learner where the error occurred and why it was incorrect, they tend merely to repeat the correct target language form. Teachers may also be inconsistent in whom they correct and which errors they correct. For example, they may correct errors made by some learners but not by others, and they may sometimes correct an error of tense but at other times ignore it. Allwright recommends a more consistent approach to error correction to avoid confusion among learners. Allwright and Bailey (1991) note that teachers often reject or correct a learner's utterance simply because it was not what they had expected to hear, which they refer to as "error of classroom discourse." They argue that these errors of classroom discourse are counterproductive and conclude that by treating errors, teachers are trying to help students move ahead in their interlanguage development; mistimed error treatment may fail to help, it may even be harmful if it is aimed at structures which are beyond the learners' stage in interlanguage development. (1991: 92)

The need for feedback on errors can also be lessened by reducing the student error rate during practice activities. Rosenshine and Stevens (1986: 383) give the following suggestions as to how this can be accomplished:

- Break down the instruction into smaller steps. Give the students instruction and practice to mastery on each step before proceeding to the next step.
- Provide the students with very explicit demonstrations on the skills whenever possible.
- Intersperse the demonstration with questions in order to maintain students' attention and to check for student understanding.
- Provide the students with teacher-monitored practice prior to seat-work activity so that the teacher can correct errors before they become part of the students' repertoire.
- With especially confusing material, provide pre-corrections by advising the students about particularly confusing areas.
- Provide sufficient independent practice – both in length and in number of exercises – to enable students to master skills to the point of overlearning (with additional exercises for the slower students).
- Re-teach the material when necessary.

Discussion

1. How useful is it for teachers to correct learners' errors? What should a teacher do when a learner repeatedly produces the same kind of error?
2. What error correction strategies have you found to be the most effective (or do you think are likely to be the most effective)?
3. Think about a group of learners you are familiar with. What do you think their beliefs and attitudes toward error correction are?

Learner language use in the classroom

Since for many language learners the classroom is the primary situation in which they have an opportunity to use the target language, the kind of language students use during lessons has an important influence on their language development. Students use the target language for a variety of different purposes within lessons, including interacting with the teacher and with other learners, and using language to negotiate and complete learning activities and assignments. One approach to understanding learner language is in terms of the communicative functions which occur during lessons. Another approach is through looking at the language needed to accomplish specific learning activities.

Communicative functions in classroom interaction

Classrooms are settings for specific kinds of transactions. Rosenshine and Stevens (1986) identify six fundamental instructional "functions."

1. Reviewing, checking previous work (and re-teaching, if necessary).
2. Presenting new content/skills.
3. Guiding student practice (and checking for understanding).
4. Giving feedback.
5. Providing independent student practice.
6. Assessing student learning.

Other researchers have focused on the communicative functions or speech acts which recur in classroom communication (Cazden, John, and Hymes 1972; Sinclair and Coulthard, 1975). Cathcart (1986) studied language use in the kindergarten class of a bilingual school in northern California and collected data on eight Spanish-speaking children in the class. She produced the following taxonomy of communicative functions to describe their language use in the class.

Taxonomy of Communicative Act Functions

Control:
  Initiate
    Call attention   "Hey, lookit."
    Request object   "Gimme that."
    Request action   "Come here."
    Invite, offer   "Do you want some?"
    Warn, threaten   "If you do, I'll . . . "

Request permission	"Can I go?"
Protest, prohibit	"Don't touch it."
Claim, assign	
Possessions	"This is mine."
Roles	"You're the daddy."
Complain	"He hit me."
Support	
Repeat, confirm	"Go on. Go on."
Add, expand	"Yes, and you too."
Clarify	"That means dog."
Intensify	"I did."
Respond	
Comply	"OK."
Refuse	"No."
Ignore	

Information:	
Announce, format initiate or	
describe	"Guess what?"
Label object	"That's a cowboy."
Label action	"He's singing."
Location	"It's over there."
Attribute	"Mine's green."
Function	"It's for writing."
Reason	"Because I found it."
State intent	"He's gonna do it."
Clarify	"I said, 'He's it.'"
Express	
Express opinion	"I like boys."
Internal state	"I feel sick."
Accompany self	"Now, I'm making tea."
Express intent	"I'm gonna fix it."
Personal experience	"We went to Mexico."
Insult, complain	"You're ugly."
Brag	"I'm bigger."
Exclaim	"Oh, no."
Request	
Request information	
Instruction	"How do you do it?"
Description	"What does a bug look like?"
Intent	"What are you gonna do?"
Request clarification	"What?"

Respond
   Give clarification   "Yeh, a green one."
   Give information
      Label object
      Label action
      Location
      Attribution
      Function
      Reason
   Deny, contradict   "I won't do it."
   Evaluate   "That's a good book."
   Shift, avoid, ignore   "I dunno."
   Imitate
   Confirm   "Yeh."

Social routine:
   Boundary markers   "Recess time"
   Politeness markers   "Thanks"
   Greetings   "Hi"

Play with language
   Sound effects   "rrrrrr"
   Word play, chants   "woo woo goo goo daa"
   "Reading"   "Once upon a time . . . "

                                 (Cathcart 1986: 137)

The kinds of functions for which learners use language within a class will vary according to the age of the learners, the content of the class, and the kinds of activities and learning arrangements that are used.

Cathcart's data illustrate another aspect of classroom learner language which has been identified by researchers (e.g., Ellis 1984), namely, the use of "formulaic speech" or "routines" to perform specific functions. Formulas are fixed patterns that are used in particular situations. Ellis (1984: 66–9) gives the following examples of formulaic speech in classroom interaction:

Situational formulas. Those associated with a specific situation: for example, "Finished" (spoken after completing a task) or "Very good" (self-congratulating in a game or classroom task).

Stylistic formulas. Those associated with a particular speech style: for example, a rather formal request such as "I wonder if I could have an eraser, please?" (said by a learner requesting goods from the teacher or another learner).

Ceremonial formulas. Those associated with ritualistic interaction: for example, "How are you?" (greeting), "Excuse me, miss" (attracting teacher's attention), or "Oh no!" (exclamation).

Gambits. Those used to organize interactions and activities: for example, "This one or that one?" (identifying nature of classroom task), "What's this?" (identifying object), "I don't know" (referring to either lack of knowledge or inability to respond), or "That's all right" (confirming course of action).

Second language acquisition researchers (e.g., Krashen and Terrell 1983) have argued that in the initial stages of language learning, many functions are expressed by such fixed expressions or formulas of the kind listed here. These can serve as useful communication strategies for learners, enabling them to manage many of the communicative demands of the classroom when they lack more complex linguistic means to do so. "Informal second language acquirers often make extensive use of routines and patterns in early stages as a means of saying things before their acquired competence is ready" (Krashen and Terrell 1983: 43). They suggest that as language development progresses, learners will make less use of formulas and produce a more varied range of sentence patterns and structures.

Language used for learning activities

As was seen in Chapter 8, teachers often select learning activities to generate particular types of interaction and language practice. Activities such as problem solving or role-play activities are used to generate communicative language use and to practice turn-taking, asking questions, and asking for clarification. A number of researchers have investigated the kind of language that learners use when completing these kinds of activities in order to answer questions such as the following:

- How effectively, despite linguistic shortcomings, can learners understand and convey a message in a second or foreign language?
- How accurate is the language they use?
- How appropriate is the language they use?
- What are their areas of deficiency (in grammar, vocabulary, appropriateness, spelling, pronunciation)?
- What strategies do they employ for coping with deficiencies?
- To what extent do they monitor their own performance and self-correct? How successful is their self-correction?

- What is the relationship between their linguistic knowledge and the communicative performance?
- How do native speakers react to their performance?

(Green and Hecht 1989: 95)

The issue of the quality of the language that learners use when completing communicative tasks has been examined in a number of studies (Day 1986; Ellis 1985). There are two dimensions to this question. One has to do with formal appropriateness (i.e. accurate grammar and pronunciation), and the other with communicative appropriacy (i.e., language that is appropriate in terms of formality versus informality, politeness, authenticity, etc.).

On the issue of grammatical accuracy, learners are sometimes observed to use grammatically inappropriate forms when completing classroom tasks such as pair or group discussion (Porter 1986). Higgs and Clifford (1982) argue that giving learners unstructured or free conversational tasks to complete without providing sufficient linguistic support may lead to the fossilization of incorrect speech (i.e., the permanent establishment of incorrect grammatical structures), particularly with less proficient learners. Porter (1986) found that learners carrying out communicative classroom tasks sometimes used forms that were sociolinguistically inappropriate, such as inappropriate ways of expressing opinion, agreement, and disagreement. "These findings . . . suggest that only native speakers (or perhaps very advanced nonnative speakers) can provide truly appropriate input that will build sociolinguistic competence" (p. 218).

Lynch (1989), however, provides the following examples of questions produced by learners at a post-elementary level of language proficiency while they worked in pairs on a task which involved marking a route on a city map. These examples show that the communicative task did indeed provide a great variety of opportunities to ask questions. The questions which the learners asked all followed the correct word order for English, although some of them lack auxiliary verbs and articles, which would be typical of learners at this stage of language development.

What to do?	National palace this one?
Are you agree to repeat?	Where is the national monument?
Right or left?	How you know it is?
Go down?	What's the name of the road?
Ibrahim, what you understand?	What is Vat road?
Turn left this one?	You hear "by bus"?
This one?	That's the national monument?

Where is pagoda?
Where is the door?
How will you know?
Which one?
Which one pagoda?
You didn't understand?
Do you want to ask teacher?
But how can you turn left?
When did you turn right?
How do you sure?
Is this explain?
Why you need to listen and make it?
National what?
Where down?
Where is monument?
From which way?

"National" – may you write?
What does "Statue" mean?
Which one market?
This one?
Clear?
Is it museum or . . . ?
Where is first left?
Where is national museum?
From which door you come out?
From this side?
Silk mill?
Do you agree to listen again?
It is in the tower?
Near factory is here?
Is factory for silk, silk mill?
Did you hear "turn right"?

(Lynch 1989: 121–2)

As this review has demonstrated, a great many factors influence both the quantity and quality of teacher talk as well as learner-generated language during instruction. Collecting and analyzing data on classroom language use is sometimes problematic since the process of obtaining such data can influence the quality of the information collected. However, since language is the means by which learners demonstrate the level of their understanding as well as the extent of their learning, an awareness of the nature of classroom language use is central to our understanding of effective language teaching.

Discussion

1. Review the list of classroom functions found in a kindergarten bilingual classroom given on pages 193–195. How many of these functions are likely to occur in other kinds of ESL classes? For what other kinds of classroom functions are learners you are familiar with likely to use English?
2. Can you give other examples of the four kinds of formulaic speech on pages 195–196? Which might be used by learners in ESL classes? Have you observed other examples of formulaic speech of this kind being used by ESL learners in language classrooms?

3. Can you give examples of communicative learning activities which could be used to generate learner production of specific language forms or functions? How can one give learners feedback on the quality of the language they use while completing communicative learning activities such as role plays or information gap tasks?

Follow-up activities

Journal activities

1. Monitor a class you are teaching or observing from the point of view of teacher–student communication. How are communication problems dealt with? What strategies do you (or the teacher) use to facilitate communication with the learners? How does this affect the quality of classroom language?
2. Describe your approach to the treatment of learner errors. Do you (or the teacher you observe) have a set of strategies, and do you (or the teacher) apply these consistently?

Investigation tasks

1. Record a lesson you teach (or observe a teacher teaching a lesson). What strategies did you (or the teacher) use to facilitate comprehension?
2. Review the lesson you recorded in question 1, focusing this time on the teacher's use of questions. Try to classify the questions into *procedural questions, convergent questions,* and *divergent questions.* What other kinds of questions occurred?
3. Prepare a set of convergent questions and a set of divergent questions that could be used during a language lesson (e.g., as part of a reading or listening lesson). Teach the class and record it. Was there any observable difference between the kind of response generated by the two different kinds of questions?
4. Interview a group of learners and find out what their beliefs about error correction are. What error correction strategies do they think are most useful?
5. Record a group of learners carrying out a communicative task (e.g., a pair or group task). Then listen to the tape and try to identify examples of the following:
   a. communication strategies

b. self-correction
c. clarification request
To what extent was the learners' language grammatically correct and communicatively appropriate?

Peer observation tasks

1. Observe a lesson and measure the wait-time of the teacher. What was the average wait-time during the lesson? Do you think the wait-time was an appropriate length to give students a chance to respond? Then invite the teacher to observe your teaching and note the wait-time during one of your lessons.
2. Observe a lesson, focusing on the strategies the teacher uses to correct learner errors. How and when did the teacher correct learner errors? Then invite the teacher to observe your teaching and note down the correction strategies you use. After the observations, discuss the effectiveness of the strategies used during the lessons.

Action research case study #7

Error correction

This was prepared by a group a teachers working in a private language school in an EFL context.

INITIAL REFLECTION

We were concerned that as a group we were unaware of how we corrected our students' errors and whether our error correction strategies were effective. Having read some of the literature on error correction, we were aware that teachers were often inconsistent in their approach to errors. We wanted to come up with workable guidelines for our teachers to follow.

PLANNING AND ACTION

We focused on teachers' responses towards learners' oral errors. We decided to videotape 15 two-hour classes at different levels. We informed students of our goals, and then arranged to video the classes. We then analyzed the data. We first reviewed the whole video, timed each activity, and counted the number of errors learners made and how many of these errors were corrected by the teacher during each activity. This information was used to find out when teachers corrected the most and when they corrected the least. We next choose those parts of the lessons where errors frequently occurred. These segments were reviewed again to determine the types of errors students made, which of these errors teachers corrected, and how teachers corrected these errors.

OBSERVATION

We found that in beginning levels the most common types of errors we corrected were related to pronouns, word order, and pronunciation. Most of these errors resulted in miscommunication; students were corrected because they were not being understood. The amount of error correction that occurred depended on the level of the class. In the pre-intermediate classes, 80% of the errors were ignored, while in the beginning and intermediate classes only 30% of the errors were ignored. We also found that we corrected less during open-ended communicative activities or unguided discussions. We discovered that the usual strategy to correct errors was to interrupt the learner and repeat the correct form. The learner would then automatically repeat what the teacher had said.

REFLECTION

These observations about how we dealt with error correction led to several discussions on the topic. Generally we agree that the types of errors we correct and the timing of the correction is appropriate. We are less happy, however, with the discovery that we seem to use a very limited repertoire of correction techniques. We have therefore examined other possible strategies for error correction and are consciously trying to implement these alternatives during our lessons. We are currently planning a second cycle of this action research project to determine if we have been able to expand our repertoire of correction strategies, and how effective these are.

Epilogue

This book reflects a different perspective on teacher development from that implicit in many TESL education programs. Traditional views of language teaching have often seen it as an applied science, that is, as "Applied linguistics." The significant theory and knowledge base underlying teaching is presented during the campus course. The teacher's job is to apply this knowledge in the classroom. Once teachers enter teaching they are expected to master the more "trivial" aspects of teaching, such as how to handle routine classroom techniques and procedures. Improvement in teaching comes about as teachers match their teaching more closely to the theories and principles introduced during their MATESL (or similar) course.

The concept of reflective teaching, however, as with other inquiry-oriented approaches to teaching, makes different assumptions about the nature of teacher development. The process of reflecting upon one's own teaching is viewed as an essential component in developing knowledge and theories of teaching, and is hence a key element in one's professional development. This process is one which continues throughout a teacher's career. Formal programs of teacher education represent only an initial, though essential, first phase in teacher development. As Zeichner (1992: 297) observes:

... learning to teach is a process that continues throughout a teacher's career and no matter what we do in our teacher education programs and no matter how well we do it, at best we can only prepare teachers to begin teaching. Consequently, teacher educators must be committed to helping prospective teachers internalize the dispositions and skills to study their teaching and to become better at teaching over time, that is, to help teachers take responsibility for their own professional development.

Throughout this book a number of important issues in language teaching and learning have been explored in order to help develop a critically reflective approach to teaching. In order to explore teaching it has been necessary to break it down into separate components, but in reality, the

202

issues discussed in the book are overlapping and interrelated. The topics included are not necessarily those which occur in standard ESL methodology courses, but serve to highlight important issues that recur in teaching at any level and in many different situations. They are also topics which are well established in the literature on teaching and for which there is a considerable research history (Wittrock 1986).

Freeman (1992a) poses the central challenge of teacher education as understanding how teachers conceive of what they do and how they adopt new ways of understanding and behaving. This cannot be achieved simply by exposing teachers to research or theory but comes about through teachers' constructing their own theories of teaching, drawing on their knowledge, skills, training, and their experience of teaching. The process of critical reflection which has been the focus of this book is one way in which this growth can come about.

References

Adams, R., and Biddle, B. 1970. *Realities of Teaching: Explorations with Video Tape*. New York: Holt, Rinehart & Winston.

Allwright, D. 1975. Problems in the study of the teacher's treatment of learner error. In M. Burt and H. Dulay (eds.), *On TESOL '75: New Directions in Second Language Learning, Teaching, and Bilingual Education*. Washington, D.C.: TESOL. pp. 96–109.

Allwright, D. 1988. *Observation in the Language Classroom*. New York: Longman.

Allwright, D., and Bailey, K. 1991. *Focus on the Language Classroom: An Introduction to Classroom Research for Language Teachers*. Cambridge: Cambridge Unversity Press.

Bailey, K.M. 1990. The use of diary studies in teacher education programs. In J.C. Richards and D. Nunan (eds.), *Second Language Teacher Education*. New York: Cambridge University Press. pp. 215–26.

Banbrook, L., and Skehan, P. 1989. Classroom and display questions. In C. Brumfit and R. Mitchel (eds.), *Research in the Language Classroom*. London: Modern English Publications in association with The British Council.

Barr, P.; Clegg, J., and Wallace, C. 1981. *Advanced Reading Skills*. Essex: Longman.

Bartlett, L. 1987. History with hindsight: curriculum issues and directions in the AMEP. In J. Burton (ed.), *Implementing the Learner-Centred Curriculum*. Adelaide, Australia: National Curriculum Resource Centre. pp. 141–55.

Bartlett, L. 1990. Teacher development through reflective teaching. In J.C. Richards and D. Nunan (eds.), *Second Language Teacher Education*. New York: Cambridge University Press. pp. 202–14.

Bartlett, L. and Butler, J. 1985. The *planned curriculum and being a curriculum planner in the Adult Migrant Education Program*. Report to the Committee of Review of the Adult Migrant Education Program, Department of Immigration and Ethnic Affairs, Canberra.

Bialystok, E. 1978. A theoretical model of second language learning, *Language Learning*. 28: 69–83.

Biggs, J.B., and Telfer, R. 1987. *The Process of Learning.* Sydney: Prentice-Hall of Australia.

Bondy, E. 1990. Seeing it their way: what children's definitions of reading tell us about improving teacher education. *Journal of Teacher Education 41,* 5: 33–45.

Breen, M., and Candlin, C.N. 1980. The essentials of a communicative curriculum in language teaching. *Applied Linguistics 1,* 2: 89–112.

Brick, J. 1991. *China: A Handbook in Intercultural Communication.* Sydney, Australia: National Centre for English Language Teaching and Research.

Brindley, G.P. 1984. *Needs Analysis and Objective Setting in the Adult Migrant Education Program.* Australia: AMES.

Brock, M., Yu, B., and Wong, M. 1992. "Journaling" together: Collaborative diary-keeping and teacher development. In J. Flowerdew, M. Brock, and S. Hsia (eds.), *Perspectives on Second Language Teacher Development.* Hong Kong: City Polytechnic of Hong Kong, pp. 295–307.

Brophy, J., and Good, T. 1986. Teacher behavior and student achievement. In M.C. Wittrock (ed.), *Handbook of Research on Teaching,* 3rd ed. New York: Macmillan. pp. 328–75.

Brown, G. 1975. *Microteaching.* New York: Methuen.

Butler J., and Bartlett, L. 1986. The active voice of teachers: curriculum planning in the AMEP. *Prospect 2,* 1: 13–28.

Cathcart, R. 1986. Situational differences and the sampling of young children's school language. In R. Day (ed.), *Talking to Learn: Conversation in Second Language Acquisition.* Rowley, Mass.: Newbury House. pp. 118–42.

Cazden, C.B.; John, V.P.; and Hymes, D. (eds.), 1972. *Functions of Language in the Classroom.* New York: Teachers College Press.

Chaudron, C. 1988. *Second Language Classrooms: Research on Teaching and Learning.* New York: Cambridge University Press.

Clark, C.M., and Yinger, R.J. 1979. Teachers' thinking. In P. Peterson and H.J. Walberg (eds.), *Research on Teaching.* Berkeley: McCutchen.

Clark, C.M., and Peterson, P.L. 1986. Teachers' thought processes. In M.C. Wittrock (ed.), *Ha dbook of Research on Teaching,* 3rd ed. New York: Macmillan. pp. 255–96.

Connell, R.W. 1985. *Teachers' Work.* Australia: George Allen & Unwin.

Cross, K.P. 1988. In search of zippers. *Bulletin of the American Association for Higher Education 40:* 3–7.

Day, R. (ed.), 1986. *Talking to Learn: Conversation in Second Language Acquisition.* Rowley, Mass.: Newbury House.

Doff, A., and Jones, C. 1991. *Language in Use: A Pre-intermediate Course.* Cambridge: Cambridge University Press.

Doyle, W. 1986. Classroom organization and management. In M.C. Wittrock (ed.), *Handbook of Research on Teaching,* 3rd ed. New York: Macmillan. pp. 392–431.

Eisner, E.W. 1967. Educational objectives: help or hindrance? *School Review 75:* 250–66.

Ellis, R. 1984. *Classroom Second Language Development.* Oxford: Pergamon Press.

Ellis, R. 1985. *Understanding Second Language Acquisition.* Oxford: Oxford University Press.

Ellis, R., and McClintock, A. 1990. *If You Take My Meaning: Theory into Practice in Human Communication.* London: Edward Arnold.

Fanselow, J.F. 1987. *Breaking Rules: Generating and Exploring Alternatives in Language Teaching.* New York: Longman.

Feiman-Nemser, S., and Floden, R.E. 1986. The cultures of teaching. In M.C. Wittrock (ed.), *Handbook of Research on Teaching,* 3rd ed. New York: Macmillan. pp. 505–26.

Findley, C., and Nathan, L. 1980. Functional language objectives in a competency based ESL curriculum. *TESOL Quarterly 14,* 2: 221–31.

Fisher, C.W.; Felby, W.; Marliane, R.; Cahen, L.; Dishaw, M.; Moore, J.; and Berliner, D. 1978. *Teaching Behaviors, Academic Learning Time, and Student Achievement: Final Report of Phases 111–113.* Begining Teacher Evaluation Study. San Francisco: Far West Laboratory for Educational Research and Development.

Freeman, D. 1992a. Language teacher education, emerging discourse, and change in classroom practice. In J. Flowerdew, M. Brock, and S. Hsia (eds.), *Perspectives on Second Language Teacher Development.* Hong Kong: City Polytechnic of Hong Kong. pp. 1–21.

Freeman, D. 1992b. Three views of teachers' knowledge. *Teacher Development – The Newsletter of IATEFL Teacher Development Group,* No. 18.

Fujiwara, B. In preparation. Planning an advanced listening comprehension elective for Japanese university students. In K. Graves (ed.), *Teacher-designed Course.*

Gall, M. 1984. Synthesis of research on teachers' questioning. *Educational Leadership 42:* 40–7.

Good, T.L., and Brophy, J. 1987. *Looking in Classrooms.* New York: Harper & Row.

Good, T.L., and Power, C. 1976. Designing successful classroom environments for different types of students. *Journal of Curriculum Studies 8:* 1–16.

Gower R., and Walters, S. 1983. *Teaching Practice Handbook: A Reference Book for EFL Teachers in Training.* London: Heineman.

Gray, A. 1991. Self-reflection and learner competence. *Carleton Papers in Applied Language Studies* 8: 22–34.

Green, P.S., and Hecht, K. 1989. Investigating learners' language. In C. Brumfit and R. Mitchel (eds.), *Research in the Language Classroom*. London: Modern English Publications in association with The British Council.

Gregory, R. 1988. *Action Research in the Secondary Schools*. London: Routledge, Chapman & Hall.

Halkes, R., and Olson, J.K. 1984. *Teacher Thinking: A New Perspective on Persisting Problems in Education*. Lisse, Netherlands: Swets & Zeitlinger.

Harmer, J. 1991. *The Practice of English Language Teaching,* new ed. London: Longman.

Hartzell, R.W. 1988. *Harmony in Conflict: Active Adaptation to Life in Present-day Chinese Society*. Taiwan: Caves Books.

Hatch, E. 1978. *Second Language Aquisition*. Rowley, Mass.: Newbury House.

Hendrickson, J.M. 1978. Error correction in foreign language teaching: recent theory, research, and practice. *Modern Language Journal 62:* 387–98.

Heuring, D.L. 1984. The revision strategies of skilled and unskilled ESL writers: five case studies. Master's thesis. University of Hawaii at Manoa.

Higgs, T., and Clifford, R. 1982. The push toward communication. In T. Higgs (ed.), *Curriculum, Competence, and the Foreign Language Teacher.* Skokie, Ill.: National Textbook.

Horwitz, E. 1987. Surveying student beliefs about language learning. In A. Wenden and J. Rubin (eds.), *Learner Strategies in Language Learning*. London: Prentice-Hall.

Hosenfeld, C. 1977. A preliminary investigation of the reading strategies of successful and non-successful second language learners. *System 5:* 110–23.

Hosenfeld, C.A.; Kirchofer, V.; Laciura, J.; and Wilson, L. 1981. Second language reading: a curricular sequence for teaching reading strategies. *Foreign Language Annals 4:* 415–22.

Hubbard, P.; Jones, H.; Thorton, B.; and Wheeler, R. 1983. *A Training Course for TEFL*. Oxford: Oxford University Press.

Hyland, K. 1991. Collaboration in the language classroom. *Prospect 7,* 1: 85–92.

Jackson, P., and Lahaderne, H. 1967. Inequalities of teacher-pupil contacts. *Psychology in the Schools* 4: 204–8.

Johnson, K. 1992a. The relationship between teachers' beliefs and practices during literacy instruction for non-native speakers of English. *Journal of Reading Behavior* 24: 83–108.

Johnson, K. 1992b. The instructional decisions of pre-service English as a second language teachers: new directions for teacher preparation programs. In J. Flowerdew, M. Brock, and S. Hsia (eds.), *Perspectives on Second Language Teacher Development.* Hong Kong: City Polytechnic of Hong Kong. pp. 115–34.

Jones, L., and von Baeyer, C. 1983. *Functions of American English.* New York: Cambridge University Press.

Kagan, S. 1987. *Cooperative Learning Resources for Teachers.* Riverside: University of California.

Keefe, J. 1979. Learning style: an overview. In A. Gregorc (ed), *Student Learning Styles.* Reston, Va.: National Association of Secondary School Principals.

Kember, D., and Kelly, M. 1992. *Using Action Research to Improve Teaching.* Hong Kong: Hong Kong Polytechnic.

Kemmis, S., and McTaggart, R. 1988. *The Action Research Planner,* 3rd ed. Victoria: Deakin University Press.

Kennedy, N. 1990. *Policy Issues in Teacher Education.* East Lansing, Mich: National Center for Research on Teacher Education.

Kessler, C. (ed.). 1992. *Cooperative Language Learning.* Englewood Cliffs, N.J.: Prentice-Hall.

Kindsvatter, R.; Willen, W.; and Ishler, M. 1988. *Dynamics of Effective Teaching.* New York: Longman.

Knowles, L. 1982. *Teaching and Reading.* London: National Council on Industrial Language Training.

Krashen, S.D. 1985. *The Input Hypothesis: Issues and Implications.* New York: Longman.

Krashen, S.D, and Terrell, T. 1983. *The Natural Approach.* Oxford: Pergamon.

Lapp, R. 1984. The process approach to writing: towards a curriculum for international students. Master's thesis. Working Paper available from Department of English as a Second Language, University of Hawaii.

Larsen-Freeman, D. 1986. *Techniques and Principles in Language Teaching.* New York: Oxford University Press.

Leki, I. 1989. *Academic Writing: Techniques and Tasks.* New York: St. Martin's Press.

Levin, T., with Long, R. 1981. *Effective Instruction.* Alexandria, Va.: Association for Supervision and Curriculum Development.

Lewis, L. 1989. Monitoring: prerequisite for evaluation. *Prospect 4,* 3: 63–79.

Littlewood, W. 1986. *Communicative Language Teaching.* Cambridge: Cambridge University Press.

Long, M.H. 1983. Native speaker/non-native speaker conversation in the second language classroom. In M.A. Clark and J.Handscombes (eds.), *On TESOL '82: Pacific Perspectives on Language Learning and Teaching.* Washington, D.C.: TESOL. pp. 207–25.

Long, M.H.; Brock, C; Crookes, G; Deike, C; Potter, L; and Zhang, S. 1984. The effect of teachers' questioning patterns and wait-time on pupil participation in public high school classes in Hawaii for students of limited English proficiency. Technical Report No. 1. Honolulu: Center for Second Language Classroom Research, Social Science Research Institute, University of Hawaii at Manoa.

Long, M.H., and Sato, C.J. 1983. Classroom foreigner talk discourse: forms and functions of teachers' questions. In H.W. Seliger and M.H. Long (eds.), *Classroom Oriented Research in Second Language Acquisition.* Rowley, Mass.: Newbury House. pp. 268–85.

Lortie, D. 1975. *Schoolteacher: A Sociological Study.* Chicago: University of Chicago Press.

Lynch, T. 1989. Researching teachers: behaviour and belief. In C. Brumfit and R. Mitchel (eds.), *Research in the Language Classroom.* Modern English Publications in association with The British Council.

Macdonald, J.B. 1965. Myths about instruction. *Educational Leadership 22:* 571–6.

McGrath, I.; Davies, S.; and Mulphin, H. 1992. Lesson beginnings. *Edinburgh Working Papers in Applied Linguistics* No. 3: 92–108.

Mehan, D. 1979. *Learning Lessons.* Cambridge: Harvard University Press.

Murphy, J.M. 1991. An etiquette for the non-supervisory observation of L2 classrooms. Paper presented at the 1st International Conference on Teacher Education, City Polytechnic of Hong Kong.

Naiman, N.; Frohlich, M.; Stern, H.; and Todesco, A. 1978. *The Good Language Learner.* Toronto: Ontario Institute for Studies in Education.

Neely, A.M. 1986. Planning and problem solving in teacher education. *Journal of Teacher Education 32,* 3: 29–33.

Nunan, D. 1988. *The Learner-Centred Curriculum.* Cambridge: Cambridge University Press.

Nunan, D. 1989a. *Understanding Language Classrooms: A Guide for Teacher-initiated Action.* Hertfordshire: Prentice-Hall.

Nunan, D. 1989b. *Designing Tasks for the Communicative Classroom.* Cambridge: Cambridge University Press.

Nuttall, C. 1982. Teaching Reading Skills in a Foreign Language. London: Heinemann

Omaggio, A. 1986. *Teaching Language in Context: Proficiency-Oriented Instruction.* Boston, Mass.: Heinle & Heinle Publishers, Inc.

O'Malley, J.M., and Chamot, A.U. 1990. *Learning Strategies in Second Language Acquisiton.* New York: Cambridge University Press.

O'Neill, M., and Reid, J.A. 1985. *Educational and Psychological Characteristics of Students Gifted in English.* Canberra, Australia: Commonwealth Schools Commission.

Oxford, R. 1990. *Language Learning Strategies: What Every Teacher Should Know.* New York: Newbury House.

Pak, J. 1986. *Find Out How You Teach.* Adelaide, Australia: National Curriculum Resource Centre.

Parker, W.C. 1984. Developing teacher's decision making. *Journal of Experimental Education 52,* 4: 220–6.

Pennington, M. 1991. Work satisfaction in teaching English as a second language. Department of English Research Report No. 5. City Polytechnic of Hong Kong.

Phillips, S.V. 1972. Participant structures and communicative competence: Warm Springs Indian children in community classrooms. In C. Cazden, V. John, and D. Hymes (eds.), *Functions of Language in the Classroom.* New York: Teachers College Press.

Porter, P. 1986. How learners talk to each other: input and interaction in task-centered discussions. In R. Day, (ed.), *Talking to Learn: Conversation in Second Language Acquisition.* Rowley, Mass.: Newbury House. pp. 220–2.

Porter, P.A.; Goldstein, L.M.; Leatherman, J.; and Conrad, S. 1990. An ongoing dialogue: learning logs for teacher preparation. In J.C. Richards and D. Nunan (eds.), *Second Language Teacher Education.* New York: Cambridge University Press. pp. 227–40.

Proett, J. and Gill, K. 1986. *The Writing Process in Action: A Handbook for Teachers.* Urbana, Illinois: National Council of Teachers of English.

Reid, J. 1987. The learning style preferences of ESL students. *TESOL Quarterly 21:* 87–103.

Richards, J.C. 1990. *The Language Teaching Matrix.* New York: Cambridge University Press.

Richards, J.C.; Ho, B.; and Giblin, K. 1992. Learning how to teach: a study of EFL teachers in pre-service training. Department of English Research Report No. 19. City Polytechnic of Hong Kong.

Richards, J.C., and Lockhart, C. 1991–1992. Teacher development through peer observation. *TESOL Journal 1,* 2: 7–10.

Richards, J.C., and Rodgers, T. 1986. *Approaches and Methods in Language Teaching: A Description and Analysis.* New York: Cambridge University Press.

Richards, J.C.; Tung, P.; and Ng, P. 1991. The culture of the English language teacher: a Hong Kong example. Department of English Research Report No. 6. City Polytechnic of Hong Kong.

Rosenshine, B., and Stevens, R. 1986. Teaching functions. In M.C. Wittrock (ed.), *Handbook of Research on Teaching,* 3rd ed. New York: Macmillan. pp. 376–91.

Rowe, M.B. 1974. Wait time and reward as instructional variables, their influence on language, logic and fate control: Part one – wait time. *Journal of Research on Science Teaching* 11: 81–94

Rubin, J. 1985. *The Language Learning Disc.* Descriptive pamphlet, Joan Rubin Associates, Berkeley, Calif.

Schinke-Llano, L. 1983. Foreigner talk in content classrooms. In H.W. Seliger and M.H. Long (eds.), *Classroom Oriented Research in Second Language Acquisition.* Rowley, Mass.: Newbury House.

Schratz, M. 1992. Researching while teaching: an action research in higher education. *Studies in Higher Education 17,* 1: 81–95.

Shannon, P. 1987. Commercial readings materials, a technological ideology, and the deskilling of teachers. *Elementary School Journal 87,* 3: 307–29.

Shavelson, R. 1973. What is the basic teaching skill? *Journal of Teacher Education 24,* 2: 144–51.

Sinclair, J., and Brazil, D. 1982. *Teacher Talk.* Oxford: Oxford University Press.

Sinclair, J., and Coulthard, M. 1975. *Towards an Analysis of Discourse.* London: Oxford University Press.

Stanley, S. 1990. Negotiating lesson content and structure. *Spoken Language in the Classroom 1.* Adelaide, Australia: Languages & Multicultural Centre.

Swan, M., and Walter, C. 1990. *The New Cambridge English Course.* Cambridge: Cambridge University Press.

Sy, B. 1991. Student learning style preferences in the EFL classroom. *Applied English Instruction and Management Colloquium Proceedings.* Taipei, Taiwan: Ming Chuan College.

Tikunoff, W. 1985a. *Developing Student Functional Proficiency: Part 1.* Gainesville: University of Florida.

Tikunoff, W. 1985b. *Applying Significant Bilingual Instructional Features in the Classroom.* Rosslyn, Va.: National Clearinghouse for Bilingual Education.

Titone, R. 1968. *Teaching Foreign Languages: An Historical Sketch.* Washington, D.C.: Georgetown University Press.

Tumposky, N. 1991. Student beliefs about language learning: a cross-cultural study. *Carleton Papers in Applied Language Studies* 8: 50–65.

Vann, R., and Abraham, R. 1990. Strategies of unsuccessful language learners. *TESOL Quarterly 24,* 2: 177–98.

Walker, D. 1985. Writing and reflection. In D. Boud, R. Keogh, and D. Walker (eds.), *Reflection: Turning Experience into Learning*. London: Kogan Page.

Wallace, M.J. 1991. *Training Foreign Language Teachers: A Reflective Approach*. Cambridge: Cambridge University Press.

White, J., and Lightbown, P. 1984. Asking and answering in ESL classes. *Canadian Modern Language Review* 40: 228–44.

Willing, K. 1988. *Learning Styles in Adult Migrant Education*. Adelaide, Australia: National Curriculum Resource Centre.

Willis, J. 1981. *Teaching English through English*. London: Longman.

Wittrock, M.C. (ed.). 1986. *Handbook of Research on Teaching*, 3rd ed. New York: Macmillan.

Wong-Fillmore, L. 1985. When does teacher talk work as input? In S. Gass and C. Madden (eds.), *Input in Second Language Acquisition*. Rowley, Mass.: Newbury House. pp. 17–50.

Woods, D. 1991. Teachers' interpretations of second language teaching curricula. *RELC Journal* 22, 2: 1–18.

Woodward, T. 1991. *Models and Metaphors in Language Teacher Training: Loop Input and Other Strategies*. Cambridge: Cambridge University Press.

Wright, T. 1987. *Roles of Teachers and Learners*. Oxford: Oxford University Press.

Zeichner, K. 1992. Rethinking the practicum in the professional development school partnership. *Journal of Teacher Education 43*, 4: 296–307.

Zornada, I., and Bojanic, S. 1988. Strategies used by competent language learners. *Learners and Language Learning: Stage 1*. Adelaide, Australia: Languages & Multicultural Centre.

Index

academic learning time, 171
action research, 12–14; case studies 69–71, 91–2, 110–2, 126–8, 157–8, 179–80, 200–1; guidelines, 27–8
action zone, 138–141, 188
Active Teaching, *see* methods and approaches
activities, 161–81; complexity, 169; types, 163–5
Adams, R. and Biddle, B., 139
Adult Migrant Education Program (Australia), 38, 100
affective activities, 165
affective strategies, 64
alienated students, 146
allocated time, 171
Allwright, D., 191
Allwright, D. and Bailey, K., 191–2
analytic learning style, 60, 61
application activities, 164–5
aptitude, perceptions of, 56
assessment activities, 165–6
assessment: of students, 165, 172; of teachers, 87–8, 95–6; self-assessment, 88
audio recordings of lessons, *see* recording lessons
Audiolingualism, *see* methods and approaches
authority-oriented learning style, 60

Bailey, K. M., 7
Banbrook, L. and Skehan, P., 185
Bartlett, L., 7, 40–1
Bartlett, L. and Butler, J., 100–1

beginnings of lessons, *see* openings of lessons
beliefs, *see* learners' beliefs, and teachers' beliefs
Bialystok, E., 52
Bondy, E., 58, 144
Breen, M. and Candlin, C. N., 103
Brick, J., 55, 107
Brindley, G. P., 34–5, 80
Brown, G., 147–8; 150–51

Cathcart, R., 193–5
ceremonial formulas, 196
Chaudron, C., 148, 183, 190
Clark, C. M. and Yinger, R. J., 81
classroom observation, *see* observation
closure of lessons, 124–5
cognitive strategies, 64
cognitive style, 59–63, 75–7; definition, 59
collaborative journal writing, *see* journals
communicating goals (to students), 115, 167–8
communicative appropriacy, 197
communicative functions, 193–5
Communicative Language Teaching, *see* methods and approaches
communicative learning style, 60, 61
compensation strategies, 64
comprehensible input, 152–3, 184
comprehension activities, 164
concrete learning style, 60
convergent questions, *see* teachers' questions

Cooperative Learning, *see* methods and approaches
correction, *see* feedback
critical reflection, 1–2, 4, 6, 202–3
cross-cultural differences, 53, 55–7, 62, 107–8, 142–4

decision making, 78–96; *(see also* evaluative decisions, interactive decisions, planning decisions)
dependent students, 145
Direct Method, *see* methods and approaches
display questions, *see* teacher's questions
divergent questions, *see* teacher's questions
Doyle, W., 121

Ellis, R., 138, 182
endings of lessons, *see* closure of lessons
error correction, *see* feedback
evaluative decisions, 87–9; relation to beliefs, 88–9

feedback, 143, 188–92, 200–1; on content, 189; on form, 189–92
feedback activities, 165
Findley, C. and Nathan, L., 83
formulaic speech, 195–6
fossilization, 197
Freeman, D., 81, 203
functions, *see* language functions in the classroom

gambits, 196
Good, T. and Power, C., 144
Good, T. L. and Brophy, J., 147, 149
Gower R. and Walters, S., 123–4
Green, P. S. and Hecht, K., 197
group work, 153–4
grouping arrangements, 146–54; related to activities, 169–70

Hatch, E., 152
Hendrickson, J. M., 189
Hosenfeld, C., 65

Hubbard, P., et al., 94, 119
Hyland, K., 103

individual work (seat work), 151
input, *see* comprehensible input
instructional routines, 120–1
interaction, 138–60; and relation to second language acquisition, 152; student-student, 44–47
interactional competence, 141–4
interactional patterns, 144–146
interactive decisions, 83–7; and relation to beliefs, 86
isolated students, 145

Johnson, K., 37, 85–6
journals, 6–8; guidelines, 7, 16–7; collaborative journal writing, 8, 18

Kindsvatter, R., Willen, W., and Isler, M., 30, 78
Knowles, L., 60
Krashen, S. D., 152, 184
Krashen, S. D. and Terrell, T., 196

language functions in the classroom, 193
language use, 182–202; of the teacher, 182–92; of the learner, 193–9
Larsen-Freeman, D., 103
learner strategies, 63–7, 69–71, 73–4; definition, 63; effective versus ineffective, 65; relation to activities, 165, 170
learner-centered approach, 34, 38, 100–1
learners' beliefs, 52–9; about English, 52–3; about learning, 55, 72; about reading, 58; about teaching, 54–5; differences between teachers and students, 35, 53–4; and relation to second language acquisition, 52
learners' goals, 56–8
learning preferences, 60–62; questionnaire, 20
learning strategies checklist, 73–4
learning style, *see* cognitive style

lesson planning, 79–83, 93–4, 161–3
lesson reports, 6, 9–10, 19, 44–7, 137, 160, 181
Levin, T. with Long, R., 171
Littlewood, W., 119
Long, M. H., 152, 153
Long, M. H. and Sato, C. J., 187
Lortie, D., 31
Lynch, T., 197

McGrath, I., Davies, S., and Mulphin, H., 115, 129
memorization activities, 164
memory strategies, 64
metacognitive strategies, 64
methods and approaches: Active Teaching, 102; Audiolingualism, 103; Communicative Language Teaching, 103, 119; Cooperative learning, 102–3; Direct Method, 101–2; Situational Language Teaching, 119; Total Physical Response, 103–4
modification of teachers' language, *see* teachers' language

needs analysis, 99
Nunan, D., 80, 100, 161, 189
Nuttall, C., 120

O'Malley, J. M. and Chamot, A. U., 65
objectives, 79–81, 83, 161
observation, 6, 12; guidelines, 22–3; forms, 140, 149–50, 159; tasks, 43, 69, 91, 110, 126, 156, 178, 200 (*see also* peer observation)
openings of lessons, 114–8, 129
Oxford, R., 63–5

pacing (of lessons), 122–124; relation to decision making, 122
pair work, 152–3
Parker, W. C., 83–4
participation, *see* student participation
peer observation, 6; guidelines, 24–6
Pennington, M., 40
perceptual learning style preference questionnaire, 75–7

phantom students, 145
Phillips, S. V., 142
planning decisions, 78–83; definition, 78
Porter, P., 197
practice activities, 163–4
presentation activities, 163
procedural questions, *see* teachers' questions
process approach to writing, *see* writing
professionalism, 40–1

questioning skills, 187–8
questionnaire forms, *see* surveys and questionnaires
questions, *see* teachers' questions

reading: lesson format, 118; sequencing, 120, 133–6; strategies, 65
recording lessons, 6, 11
referential questions, *see* teachers' questions
Richards, J. C., 88, 123
Richards, J. C. and Rodgers, T., 103
roles of teachers, 97–112; and approach or method, 101–4; and culture, 107–9; and institutional factors, 98–101; and personal view, 104–7; definition of, 97
Rosenshine, B. and Stevens, R., 114, 115, 192–3
Rubin, J., 66

Schinke-Llano, L., 139
self-inquiry, 3
sequencing of lessons, 118–22, 130–6
Shavelson, R., 78
situational formulas, 195
Situational Language Teaching, *see* methods and approaches
social strategies, 64–5
social students, 145
Stanley, S., 91
strategies, *see* learner strategies
strategy activities, 165
structuring, 113–37
student participation, 187–8

students' beliefs, *see* learners' beliefs
stylistic formulas, 195
surveys and questionnaires, 6, 10, 20–1, 48–9, 50–1, 72, 73–4, 75–7

task-oriented students, 145
teacher talk, 184
teacher decision making, *see* decision making
teachers' beliefs, 29–51; about English, 32–3; about language teaching as a profession, 40–1; about learning, 34–6, 50–1; about reading, 58; about teaching, 36–8, 48–9; about the program and curriculum, 38–9; differences between teachers and students, 35, 53–4; sources, 30–2
teachers' language, 182–5; (*see also* teacher talk)
teachers' questions, 185–8; convergent, 186–7; display, 187; divergent, 187; procedural, 186; purposes of, 185; referential, 187

Tikunoff, W., 102, 123
time on task, 171
Total Physical Response, *see* methods and approaches
transitions within lessons, 121–2
Tumposky, N., 56–7
two-way and one-way tasks, 152

Vann, R., and Abraham, R., 63, 65
video recordings of lessons, *see* recording lessons

wait time, 188
Wallace, M. J., 96–7
whole-class teaching, 147–51
Willing, K., 60–2, 74
Wong-Fillmore, L., 113, 114, 118, 120
Woods, D., 86, 88
Wright, T., 98
writing: strategies, 65; process approach, 119–20, 132

Zeichner, K., 202

19-07-85